Evolution: Really?

*A Christian Humanist Inquiry Into a
Persistent Controversy*

Richard Terrell

WestBow
PRESS
A DIVISION OF THOMAS NELSON

WestBow Press books may be ordered through booksellers or by contacting:

WestBow Press
A Division of Thomas Nelson
1663 Liberty Drive
Bloomington, IN 47403
www.westbowpress.com
1-(866) 928-1240

Because of the dynamic nature of the Internet, any web addresses or links contained in this book may have changed since publication and may no longer be valid. The views expressed in this work are solely those of the author and do not necessarily reflect the views of the publisher, and the publisher hereby disclaims any responsibility for them.

Any people depicted in stock imagery provided by Thinkstock are models, and such images are being used for illustrative purposes only.

Certain stock imagery © Thinkstock.

ISBN: 978-1-4497-1351-5 (sc)
ISBN: 978-1-4497-1350-8 (e)

Library of Congress Control Number: 2011923626

Printed in the United States of America

WestBow Press rev. date: 5/18/2011

Contents

Introduction

"I don't understand why we've got so many students who don't believe in evolution." The statement, offered by a faculty colleague, carried with it an undertone of puzzlement mixed with a sense of danger. On another occasion a different colleague remarked about some students she had encountered in a first-year liberal arts seminar. "They don't accept evolution." The tone of this statement combined a kind of dumb-founded amazement with a clearly communicated irritation. "They're so *narrow minded!*"

The reflections I set forth in the following discussion may also earn me the raised eyebrow. There are some things that are just not to be questioned in academic life, and the doctrine of evolution is one of them. The question, however, is not why first-year students are slow to receive evolutionary enlightenment but why so many professionals in various fields of science question it. That they do, and in fact have done so ever since the advent of Darwinism in the later nineteenth century, is readily apparent to anyone who looks into it and gives a fair hearing to different points of view.

This book has its origins in a paper I wrote for the benefit of Christian students in 1975 on the campus where I was teaching. At the time, I was responding to the situation of a dedicated Christian student—a young woman—who was majoring in biology with a view to acquiring public school teaching certification. Christine related to me a troubling statement made to her by one of her biology professors. The professor had advised her that she should not aspire to teach biology in the public schools by reason of her Christian faith. My indignation at this kind of academic malpractice spurred me to do some research into the alleged "warfare" between science and religion, and the result was the discussion that forms the bulk of what follows. I have, however, integrated more recent materials to reflect the character and current nature of the larger discussion that continues in our society. Clearly, the issues and arguments have evolved significantly over the ensuing decades. Nevertheless, many of the arguments heard today still reflect classic arguments set forth by the older voices. For example, does Stephen Hawking's view of origins, as stated in his 2010 bestseller *The Grand Design,* add anything fundamentally different from the viewpoint of Bertrand Russell that we are all mere "accidental collocations of atoms?"

The professor cited above may be an extreme case, although my own sense is that his attitude is more prevalent than academic leaders might care to admit. It is also likely that significant numbers in the professoriate beyond the natural sciences share his perspectives. Psychology and sociology come most readily to mind in this regard. Students are the recipients of such thinking, which may be communicated in overt or subtle ways by people with advanced degrees and toward whom students have a natural relationship and loyalty. In this context, students can easily develop the notion that there is an irrevocable divide between their religious faith commitments and the open, joyful pursuit of learning.

Another anecdote lying behind my interest in pursuing these matters finds me in the college sculpture studio. On this occasion I was engaged in a conversation with a very sharp, intellectually inclined student who maintained an aggressively confident stance as an atheist. Rich held that belief in God and the specific doctrines of Christianity were without merit. In his view, the Christian vision lacked logical coherence and evidential support. Our conversations on this topic were typically long, energetic, and exhausting. Conversely, they were also exhilarating. On this particular day our discussion lasted nearly two hours, but never once did science or specifically Darwinian thought become an issue. When Rich left, a young woman who had been making pottery in the adjoining studio approached me. "Mr. Terrell," she said, "that discussion was really interesting. I found it fascinating. But I have one question. What about . . . well, what about *evolution?*"

The question was almost shocking, as it demonstrated how difficult it is to imagine any discussion of the "God question" without first addressing the subject of evolution. Had Rich and I been negligent? Indeed, it does seem that these days one cannot discuss the issues of theology, faith, Christ, morality, etc., without first taking a bow to Charles Darwin. Even many people who embrace Christian belief find it necessary to seek some degree of reconciliation with Darwinian thought. This is to a certain degree appropriate, for there is no question as to the influence of Darwinian concepts upon the practice of modern science and, in fact, the shaping of the larger philosophical outlook and worldview of "modern man."

I have no problem working through objections to the God thesis that are grounded in Darwinian evolution. I do insist, however, that science does not legitimately possess the sole, privileged prerogative to make pronouncements on issues of human origins, human nature, and human destiny. Philosophers, theologians, and maybe even artists have something to day about all this. Moreover, I affirm that they offer more than mere opinion but that they bring *knowledge* to the discussion. This being so, I insist that the larger discussion calls upon a broad range of insights from various disciplines, including the disciplines of the humanities.

My discussion will no doubt meet with disinterested dismissal by some, skepticism or patronizing indulgence in others, and even indignation in those who regard all questions to be settled. I am, after all, someone whose "credential" is in the arena of the visual arts. What do artist's know, anyway? (I'm recalling, here, a suggestion made by an academic colleague that art is a "non-cognitive activity.") But before passing judgment or assuming that I'm about to cut off my ear, at least consider the arguments. They represent the broad range of thought that is expressed by critical thinkers representing the arts and humanities as well as the sciences. I hope the reader will at least come to a deeper understanding as to why, after over a century of Darwinian acceptance, countless individuals of reasonable intelligence, high education, and yes even scientific training, do not bow the knee to the long bearded Brit whose observations of some finches on the Galapagos Islands radically changed the entire worldview of a civilization. Mostly, however, I hope that this essay will be of some encouragement to people like Christine.

There are certain limited contours of my concern that I must emphasize. First and most importantly, I am primarily concerned with the notion (a conceit, actually) that the question of God is not worthy of consideration *because of* evolutionary concepts in the realm of science, especially biology. Science, *qua* science, has nothing of an authoritative nature to say about the question of God, despite the insistence of writers like Richard Dawkins (*The God Delusion*) or Stephen Hawking (*The Grand Design*) that it does. Scientists may contribute to that question, but that question is much greater than science. The theist does not have to make prior answer to evolution in order to speak. The practice of insisting that theists do so (usually by scientists who adopt a fashionable atheism on the basis of their science) is open to challenge, and that challenge necessitates a critique of evolution itself. To undertake this is risky business, especially for someone in the realm of academe, for there is no intellectual field more given to condemnation of others, intellectual ridicule, professional intimidation, and just irritable indignation than that of the established narrative upholding the "sure fact" and necessary acknowledgment of evolution and Darwin's triumph.

Someone may ask how any sane person can deny that creatures adapt to their environment, that genetic change occurs, and that species flourish, struggle, die off, or that nature reveals structural relationships between living forms. These are evident *facts!* This challenge is welcome, for it invites a clarification as to what we are *not* talking about in this discussion. The answer to this is simply that nobody *is* denying these realities. Not only is this objection a classic "straw man" argument, tactically introduced in the interests of characterizing Darwin's skeptics as intellectually backward know-nothings, it represents an evasion of the real issues. These issues are philosophic and historical in nature, having to do with the larger scenario of evolution or what is often referred to as *macroevolution*. This is the realm that holds all the controversy, and it is this arena that calls for insight from the humanist, the artist, the theologian, the scientist, and even offerings from plain common sense (although in a world of quantum physics, common sense does seem to lose some of its authority).

Thus, we always keep in mind the useful distinction between *microevolution* (observable change in nature) and the larger umbrella of *macroevolution* (the broad historical and universal vision). In the discussion that follows, when I am referring to a critique of evolution, I have in mind the "big picture" evolution, or macroevolution and its expansive worldview known as *evolutionism*.

Additionally, I am not terribly concerned with attempts to synthesize theology with evolutionary science. "Theistic evolutionists" may feel comfortable with their blending of Christian concepts with evolutionary ideas, but such attempts tend to receive a bored disdain from the real Darwinians. Other forms of "spiritual evolutionism" as seen in today's "New Age" movement are also on the outer boundary of my concern, except to say that they offer clear and powerful evidence that evolution is, for a great many people who embrace it, much more than a scientific theory. Indeed, one might argue that in regard to the New Age spirituality, evolution is a spiritual doctrine. This became readily apparent to me a few years ago upon visiting the library of the American Theosophical Society in Wheaton, Illinois. There, the entrance displayed a large mural meant to illustrate human spiritual destiny. The imagery was that of the classic Darwinian evolution-of-life scenario of life progressing from primordial, primitive creatures to humanity. The culmination of this vision was expressed in the arrival of a glowing, human-like being, representative of what looked like an image of superhumanity.

I will seek to establish some clarity to the issues by focusing on the most extreme position, the one that fuels the new, recent assault on theism from such writers as Richard Dawkins but which reflect and recapitulate the older visions of writers like Bertrand Russell or Julian Huxley. This is the position of hard materialism, the declaration that nature is all there is, that the evolutionary theory explains everything that needs to be explained, and that in the final analysis everything that we find precious and meaningful in life reduces to what Russell called the "accidental collocation of atoms." This view of life is raised up for our acceptance as being *necessitated* by science—science empowered and guided by the grand, all-embracing idea of evolution. As classic promoters of Darwinian evolution have alleged, the concept of divine creation runs counter to the whole arena of scientific inquiry.

Really?

Despite such dogmatism in the name of science (more properly identified by the concept of *scientism*), questions about the efficacy and evidential strength of Darwinian evolution persist, to the puzzlement and dismay of most academic teachers in the sciences. For the scientific layperson, though, we might appreciate that even Darwinists themselves admit that the idea of evolution is counter-intuitive to normal human perception. Richard Dawkins himself tells us that scientists study natural structures that "seem" to have been designed but which, against all natural sense, are really not.

No doubt the biggest reason for skepticism regarding the evolutionary doctrine, however, is the arrogant pose taken by prominent people while ridiculing, in the name of science, the collective apprehension of humanity of a transcendent order that is manifest in the workings of the natural world. To listen to leading atheist evolutionists is to encounter a blanket indictment of virtually all believers in a transcendent order as "superstitious," as "medieval," as "anti-intellectual," or as people whose minds are little more than reproductive molds cast from the bumpkin character of Matthew Brady in the historically twisted drama *Inherit the Wind*.

This essay is, then, a focused critique of an idea that claims universal authority in human life in regard to which we must understand everything, from bodily processes to ethics. I do not have any intention of "proving" the existence of the Judeo-Christian God. I am fully aware that even if my critique were to prove infallible and convincing, such effort would not, in itself, establish anything concerning the credibility of theistic belief in general or the Christian faith in particular. Theistic belief, either of a general or specifically Christian character, presents its own issues of faith, reason, and evidence, but that is another discussion altogether. What I do have in mind, though, is to demonstrate that the grand idea of evolution should not stand in the way of anyone's theistic commitments. Allowing it to do so, or advocating that it should do so, is simply presumptuous.

One might argue that I am simply setting up a "straw man," for certainly not all scientists are militant atheists in the mold of Richard Dawkins and other so-called new atheists. This is true but it is really beside the point. Historians of ideas readily acknowledge that Darwinian evolution is an idea in modern intellectual life that has done as much or more than any other concept to influence the secularization of society and even theology itself. It has been continually promoted as an idea to which every idea of human origin, meaning, and destiny must pay dues. Others may want to back off, and say something like "Oh, that's just Dawkins." Dismissal, though, is so very uninteresting and merely evasive. We are dealing with major thinkers of much influence in these matters.

Which leads me to another observation that may play a role in the layperson's perception of the controversy over evolution. This is the claim, often offered by way of retreating from the unease of discussing these issues, that "people just don't understand evolution; they are ignorant of what it is." This perception can be linked to the scientists' *mea culpa* that they have "just not done a very good job of explaining it." Yet, as the following arguments will seek to demonstrate, materialistic evolutionism does not make sense to a significant number of people who are trained in the sciences—both hard and soft—who need no further "explanations." Students have a right to approach the issues in a spirit of free and open inquiry. This is the task to which the following discussion seeks to contribute.

Readers please note that footnote references are continuous through both major parts of this book. I have included three book reviews in appendices that explore in a more focused way issues raised in the body of the discussion, as these issues are presented in representative books.

Richard Terrell, Lincoln, NE
January, 2011

Part I

Evolutionism as a Worldview: Aspects of History and Myth

"Clearly, there is more than science in Darwinism. The chief additional ingredient is a craving for the absence of metaphysical perspectives, a craving which should not be left immune to scrutiny."

— Stanley L. Jaki (*The Road of Science and the Ways to God*)

In a semi-darkened auditorium, a blaze of light illuminated a stage against which I could observe the silhouetted shapes of the heads of other audience members. Enraptured, we were listening to the music of Beethoven as performed by the St. Louis Symphony. I imagine that others, like myself, occasionally felt physical sensations streaming through their bodies linked to stirrings of mind and emotion, visual images, or scenarios of adventure, love, conflict, danger, resolution, or other evocations.

At some point I found myself thinking, quite unexpectedly, about Darwinism. I asked myself a question: "How does one explain this occasion, or any similar occasion, from a purely materialistic frame of reference?" I tried to put myself in that context and realized that such an exercise would necessarily have to reduce everything down to purely physical and chemical phenomena. And *that* thought struck me as absurd. Years later I came across a statement by the nineteenth-century English cleric John Henry Newman, and his words renewed the thoughts I had experienced during the symphony:

> Is it possible that that inexhaustible evolution and disposition of notes, so rich yet so simple, so intricate yet so regulated, so various yet so majestic, should be a mere sound, which is gone and perishes? Can it be that those mysterious stirrings of heart, and keen emotions, and strange yearnings after we know not what, and awful impressions from we know not whence, should be wrought in us by what is unsubstantial, and comes and goes, and begins and ends in itself? It is not so; it cannot be. No, they have escaped from some higher sphere; they are the outpourings of eternal harmony in the medium of created sound; they are echoes from our Home; they are the voice of Angels, or the Magnificat of Saints, or the living laws of Divine Governance, or the Divine Attributes; something are they besides themselves, which we cannot compass, which we cannot utter,—though mortal man, and he perhaps

not otherwise distinguished above his fellows, has
the gift of eliciting them.[1]

I was experiencing what we might call a "worldview moment,"
an event that brings into focus a contemplation of deeper meaning,
a connection with something larger than the event itself, something
suggesting a broader coherence and significance and explanatory
principle. My perception was that a purely materialistic outlook
and understanding of human life lacked *explanatory power* for the
phenomenon observed. An explanation from that point of view
would amount to endless special pleading and inventive twists. That
materialistic worldview was, in my judgment, inadequate to the
occasion. Newman's beautiful, poetic questioning of such an event
seems to make a connection that is coherent, rational, and clear.
We are transported by such music because its ultimate source is
transcendent, intelligent, and beautiful in itself.

Any discussion of the real or imagined conflicts between science
and Christian faith leads necessarily to a consideration of "worldview."
Our initial task, then, is to arrive at a basic understanding of what
a worldview is, and to contrast the fundamental aspects of the
Christian worldview with that of evolutionism.

What is a Worldview?

A worldview is a way of interpreting experience. A person's
worldview is formed from many influences, from immediate
observations of objects and events to the awareness of cultural
tradition. Worldviews also are shaped by the role played by
presuppositions, or the given assumptions that guide interpretive
responses to reality. Every system of thought or spirituality/religion
has its presuppositions. The fundamental presupposition of the
Christian faith is stated in Genesis—that in the beginning of the
world, God created the heavens and the earth. If that presupposition
is taken away, nothing else about the Christian faith makes sense. In

---

1   Cited by Thomas Dubay, S.M., in *The Evidential Power of Beauty: Science
and Theology Meet* (San Francisco: Ignatius Press, 1999), 57.

fact, in such a case the record and witness concerning Jesus Christ would become a gross absurdity.

Scientific materialism—or the worldview of "hard naturalism,"—rejects the Christian presupposition of divine creation. It is a way of thinking that begins with the assumption that there is no God, or that if there is the deity is not accessible to human reason and intelligence. Clearly, the two stances are incompatible and cannot be reconciled. The universe is either the result of a designing intelligence or it is not. If that designer/creator is denied *in the name of science,* then a Christian must show reason for dissenting from that view.

According to the biblical view, God is knowable and interacts with humanity through real events and circumstances that reveal his character and purposes. The crowning event of this revelation is the life, death, and resurrection of Jesus. The Christian worldview is one shaped by the concepts of creation, fall, and redemption. In the Christian worldview, nature does not presently exist according to the original divine goodness declared in Genesis. Rather it is twisted, distorted, and "fallen" as a result of sin. The divine intention is to redeem the creation and to re-establish an unsullied goodness. Humanity's story plays a central role in this project. Our purpose here is not to explore all the theological nuances of this narrative, but to make the point that nature, in the biblical worldview, exists in a condition that awaits the realization of a divine act of recovery, or salvation (Rom. 8).

It is not the intent of biblical faith to make a scientific analysis of the world. The central concern is to state humanity's moral condition and to reveal what God promises to do about it. This is not to say, however, that scientific work has no legitimate point of contact with biblical understandings or that Christians have no legitimate purposes in scientific inquiry. If human beings embody the "image of God," as Genesis states, then it is important to understand human emotions and intelligence as completely as we can, as well as our capacities for creativity. If God created the heavens and the earth, then why should the Christian not seek to understand the processes and energies operating in the universe? Scientific concerns can have a profound meaning for the Christian, especially in view of the biblical role given to humanity to care for and exercise stewardship of the natural world. When we view things in this manner, we can see how the Christian worldview provides a real basis for a unity of knowledge and concern embracing the natural sciences, humanities and the arts, as well as a framework for exploring the ultimate meaning of life. This meaning, while including the fruition of human potential, points beyond humanity to the relationship between creator and creature.

To explore such considerations further would take us beyond the scope of this discussion into considerations of the nature of revelation. Nevertheless, I do want to stress that faith, as found in the biblical tradition, is linked to evidences. It is not the "blind faith" that many skeptics of religion envision. In fact, it is precisely in the matter of evidence that the Christian faith, which is rooted in historical settings and events, appeals to scientists with more strength than other religious traditions.

The worldview of evolutionism

In the twentieth century the Christian understanding of humanity and the universe has had to confront a significantly different worldview, that of evolutionism. Although evolutionism is not necessarily synonymous with scientific materialism the two are strongly related. Whereas evolutionism has theistic interpretations, as exemplified in the thought of Teilhard de Chardin and "process" theologians, our discussion is only peripherally concerned with these systems and will focus on evolutionism in its distinctively non-theistic posture. Christianity can get along *with* or *without* evolutionary concepts. Materialism (or metaphysical naturalism), however, is absolutely dependent upon evolutionary thought and is built upon it.

Although the scientific theory of organic evolution is to be distinguished from the overall philosophic implications of evolution*ism,* it is nevertheless true that it is difficult in many instances to keep them apart. This is because any particular belief about the origin of life and humanity leads inevitably to broader conclusions concerning the human ethical, social, and spiritual condition. The materialist denies the activity of God in creation. Nevertheless, the hardcore naturalist is still responsible for addressing questions regarding life's origins and its rich variety and complexity in non-theistic terms. The theory of evolution provides the principle whereby materialists seek to accomplish the task. Furthermore, materialists cannot escape the implications of evolution in relation to issues of human nature and destiny. Hence, a broad and totalistic worldview grows naturally from the groundwork of evolutionary theory, becoming much more than science itself.

The noted paleontologist and propagandist for evolutionism, George Gaylord Simpson, envisioned this worldview:

> Man is a glorious and unique species of animal. The species originated by evolution, it is still actively evolving, and it will continue to evolve. Future evolution could raise man to superb heights as yet hardly glimpsed, but it will not automatically do so. As far as can now be foreseen, evolutionary degeneration is at least as likely in our future as is further progress. The only way to ensure a progressive evolutionary future for mankind is for man himself to take a hand in the process.[2]

Some important ideas come through in this statement. First, one might note a kind of "salvation concern" implied. Will humanity survive? Simpson seems to leave the door open for the possibility that man may revert to some form of subhuman existence. Clearly, there are eschatological (or "final") implications. Interestingly, inevitable progress—a notion that at one time was widely accepted among evolutionists—is denied. Simpson indicates an alternative to that view.

The second crucial idea here is that man is called upon to take a hand in directing the process of evolution to ensure against evolutionary "degeneration." The implications of this are best understood within the context of evolutionism's vision of evolution

---

2   George Gaylord Simpson, *This View of Life* (New York: Harcourt, Brace and World, 1964), 285.

as the universal cosmic process itself. Julian Huxley, in *Evolution in Action,* a classic presentation of the worldview of evolutionism, indicated that there are three phases in the general process of evolution, these being the *inorganic* (the cosmological), the *organic* (biological), and the *human* (psycho-social). These three phases are interrelated and interdependent.[3] Huxley presents humanity as an evolved agent capable of directing the cosmic process. This idea has been sustained in the writings of evolutionists in the decades since his book appeared. As some evolutionists see it, man is a creature in which evolution—the cosmic process— becomes conscious of itself. It is not difficult to discern the theological implications of this. Man becomes a kind of god, guiding the universal cosmic process of creation. From the Christian point of view, it is a case of negating the creator while exalting the creature, a process that lies at the root of the Bible's definition of "idolatry."

Something akin to the Christian doctrine of the final things is in view for evolutionism's major voices, and their rhetoric sounds, at times, unabashedly "prophetic." Huxley envisioned nothing less than a "naturalistic belief system" rooted in scientific knowledge concerning "all aspects of destiny."[4] More spectacular are the words of William Day, author of *Genesis on Planet Earth* (1979), who envisions the coming of "Omega man" who will "transcend to new dimensions of time and space beyond our comprehension—as much beyond our imagination as our world was to the emerging eucaryotes." In Day's view, present-day humanity is but an intermediate creature between the lower primates and the Omega man. "What comprehension and powers over Nature Omega man will command can only be suggested by man's image of the supernatural." In accordance with the notion that humanity is evolution become conscious of itself, he proclaims that Omega man will not simply evolve naturally, but will actually be created by man.[5]

---

3   Julian Huxley, *Evolution in Action* (New York: Harper and Row, 1953; Signet edition 1957), 10.

4   Julian Huxley, *Religion Without Revelation* (New York: New American Library, Mentor edition 1958), 63

5   Mary Midgley, "The Religion of Evolution" in John Durant, ed., *Darwin and Divinity* (Oxford: Basil Blackwell, 1985), 156-157

Within this system of thought there is no room whatsoever for such Christian ideas as individual salvation, a broken and fallen world, and eternal life. The only *ultimate* meaning in a person's life is to contribute to the ongoing activity of evolution, an activity that becomes the standard of value for human thought and action. Huxley, for example, writes of the "morality of evolutionary direction."[6] Accordingly, anything that promotes the evolutionary development of humanity is good, while anything that restricts or hinders it is wrong. Certain sociopolitical implications come forth as well. Evolution stresses change in populations rather than individual entities. So, "among the values [Huxley] derives at least in part from the trend and character of evolution are intelligence, self-awareness, cooperation, and the importance of the group rather than the individual."[7] The latter point would indicate an "evolutionary morality" pointing in the direction of some form of collectivism.

Clearly, such ideas are no more scientific than those that make up the Christian worldview, which is grounded in the recognition of divine creation and humanity's accountability to the creator. Yet, it is claimed in behalf of this system of thought that it is more in accord with scientific reality and objective knowledge. It is therefore superior to traditional concepts growing out of the Christian vision. Given the prestige accorded to modern science, such a claim has a strong impact.

Evolutionary Ethics?

Not all evolutionists are as confident as Huxley was that evolution could provide a basis for ethical and moral life. Simpson, for example, does not agree with this idea. He holds that it is futile to search for ethical criteria in processes occurring before ethics themselves came into being in human life. Also, we find an interesting objection to evolutionary ethics in the thought of T.H. Huxley, Julian's grandfather. According to the elder Huxley, cosmic evolution may teach us something of how good and evil tendencies

---

6   Huxley, *Evolution in Action*, 129.

7   Ian Barbour, *Issues In Science and Religion* (New York: Harper Torchbooks, 1971), 410.

in man came about, but it is incompetent to provide a basis for deciding why a conceived "good" is preferable to what we call "evil." The geneticist Theodosius Dobzhansky recognized this problem as a critical deficiency in evolutionism's worldview, a recognition that may have been aided by Dobzhansky's dual commitment to both Darwinian evolution and Orthodox Christianity. He wrote that "evolutionary ethics have not been formulated yet, and one may reasonably doubt that they can be made scientifically convincing or aesthetically satisfying."[8]

Nor is Richard Dawkins' updated attempt to root human "goodness" in natural selection impressive. He attempts to avoid moral absolutism by positing a genetically rooted "consequentialism," which suggests a flexible morality guided by a consideration for an action's consequences.[9] Dawkins seems to be unaware that in order to do so there must be some absolute standard by which to judge the consequences as being either "good" or "bad." Dawkins actually demonstrates a rather typical fault in attempts at evolutionary ethics. Advocates of a secular and materialistic worldview smuggle traditional moral ideas derived from religion into their own system, claiming such principles as compassion and love as their own, as if they had been discovered by science. A particularly amusing example of this is Richard Carrier's citing of "love" as the core to the meaning of life in evolutionary perspective, as if the whole idea were born from natural selection.[10] (Even then, his notion of love is very clearly self-centered and dependent for its effective practice on the existence of a society with adequate technological development and leisure time in which to flourish. It lacks, then, any real universality.)

While Dawkins seems to think that human morality is rooted in genes and natural selection, atheist writer Sam Harris is more cautious, citing the possibility that much that is "natural" in human nature is at odds with what is "good."

---

8   Theodosius Dobzhansky, *Evolution, Genetics, and Man* (New York: John Wiley and Sons, Inc., 1955), 378.

9   See Richard Dawkins, *The God Delusion* (Boston: Houghton Mifflin Company, 2006), 241-267.

10 See Richard Carrier, "Our Meaning in Life," *The Secular Web* (http://www. secweb.infidels.org/?kiosk=articles&id=113)

> Appeals to genetics and natural selection can take
> us only so far, because nature has not adapted us to
> do anything more than breed. From the point of
> view of evolution, the best thing a person can do
> with his life is have as many children as possible. .
> . . From my genome's point of view, nothing could
> be more gratifying than the knowledge that I have
> fathered thousands of children for whom I now bear
> no financial responsibility.[11]

Such "scientific" approaches to questions of morality hardly seem like improvements over the Ten Commandments. The ambiguous nature of evolutionary approaches to morality and ethics is seen in the various applications of evolutionism to human life and conduct. Evolution has been used variously to support benevolent social action, *laissez-faire* economics, personal altruism, eugenics, Marxism, Nazism, and Stalinism. Take your choice.

The one absolute would seem to be that of "evolutionary progress." Simpson speaks of man's "evolutionary objectives" and of human control of our "evolutionary destiny." He makes it clear that this will involve some form of genetic manipulation.

> Control of human evolution, by any conceivable
> means, must involve some measure of control over
> human reproduction both in quantity and in quality.
> . . . It is possible to imagine some first steps, such as
> social or economic penalties against large families in
> the population as a whole and by rewards for large
> families in elite, genetically superior groups.[12]

We should understand that Simpson, writing in 1964, is advocating eugenics. As such, he confirms the charge that the early twentieth-century practice of eugenics is not, as some hold, a "misinterpretation" of Darwin but that it represents its consistent

---

11   Sam Harris, *The End of Faith* (New York: W.W. Norton and Company, 2004), 186.
12   Simpson, 285.

application in the realm of social policy. In this same discussion Simpson says that strict dictation, without concern for the consent of the reproducers, would achieve these evolutionary goals. However, such a solution would be considered unethical (although on what grounds he does not make clear). Huxley also waxed rhapsodic over the prospects of eugenics, making it a centerpiece of what he openly posited as a *religion of evolutionary humanism*.[13] Reading his words today is not so different than experiencing the Third Reich's own expectations of "improving" the human race through eugenics and purging humanity of "life unworthy of life." One wonders what there might be in evolutionary ethics to prevent such abuses as were practiced with a vengeance only a few short years before Huxley authored and published his book.

Indeed, the ethical and moral implications of the cosmic understandings of the French biologist Jacques Monod are equally troubling. Monod attributes human origins to the universe's "Monte Carlo game," and draws the following conclusion:

> [Man must] wake out of his millenary dream; and in doing so, wake to his total solitude, his fundamental isolation. Now does he at last realize that, like a gypsy, he lives on the boundary of an alien world. A world that is deaf to his music, just as indifferent to his hopes as it is to his suffering or his crimes. . . . The ancient covenant is in pieces; man knows at last that he is alone in the universe's unfeeling immensity, out of which he emerged only by chance. His destiny is nowhere spelled out, nor is his duty.[14]

---

13 Huxley, *Evolution in Action*, 132-133.
14 Jacques Monod, *Chance and Necessity*, trans. by Austryn Wainhouse (New York: Knopf, 1971), 172-180.

Is evolutionism coherent?

The relativism inherent in evolutionism has serious intellectual and moral implications. A powerful critique of these implications is found in the work of theologian Langdon Gilkey. Writing in *Religion and The Scientific Future,* Gilkey points out that the hope of creative control of human destiny through scientific knowledge is based on man's successful application of engineering, biological, and medical knowledge to nature. But control over humanity itself on a social scale is an entirely different and dangerous matter.

Gilkey sees that the secularity of modern life has caused humanity to seek the understanding of life solely within the context of finite physical and historical relationships. Consequently, the sacred has tended to vanish from the objective environment of human life. The intellectual issue is how humanity, operating solely within a context of historical contingency and moral relativism, can presume to direct human destiny. The idea of a contingent species—humanity—directing its own destiny is radically paradoxical.

> A myth which promises to man freedom *over* necessitating destiny on the basis of man's complete subservience *to* necessitating determination is surely *less* intelligible than are even the most sharply paradoxical theological accounts of the puzzles of human freedom and divine grace.[15]

The contradiction is that humanity, according to evolutionism, is the product of mindless and therefore purposeless activity. Except for the preservation of life itself, evolution does not strive to accomplish any particular purpose.[16] According to Bertrand Russell's famous formulation, stated in his remarkable essay *A Free Man's Worship,* all is but an "accidental collocation of atoms." If this is so, then how can we be certain of anything, including the necessity and strategy of

15 Langdon Gilkey, *Religion and The Scientific Future* (New York: Harper and Row, 1970), 82.
16 Dobzhansky, *Evolution, Genetics, and Man,* 374.

conducting our evolutionary destiny? The Christian apologist C.S. Lewis posed the problem in an essay:

> If my mind is a product of the irrational—if what seems my clearest reasonings are only the way in which a creature conditioned as I am is bound to feel—how shall I trust my mind when it tells me about Evolution? . . . The fact that some people of scientific education cannot by any effort be taught to see the difficulty, confirms one's suspicion that we here touch a radical disease in their whole style of thought.[17]

Stanley Jaki, a prominent historian and philosopher of science, has also clarified the contradiction that lies at the heart of the evolutionistic worldview. Of all the difficulties in Darwinism, the most fundamental one is the whole issue of *purpose*. Jaki observes that writers like Jacques Monod and other evolutionist proponents have attempted to strip nature of teleology, purpose, and design, even though there is nothing about the concept of natural selection in itself that would demand such an interpretation. Nevertheless, that purely materialistic interpretation was comfortable to what the secularizing world of the later nineteenth century was looking for. He observes the ironies of writers like Monod, T.H. Huxley, and other evolutionists devoting their entire professional lives to the purpose of showing that there is no purpose. "As Whitehead remarked of all such men of science, they 'constitute an interesting subject for study.' "[18]

We may see, then, that the premises of evolutionism lead us to intellectual contradiction as well as the moral and social dangers implied in Simpson's vision. Yet even though the worldview of evolutionism leaves humanity to operate in an intellectual and moral wasteland, we must see the significance of the attempt to conceive

---

17 C.S. Lewis, "The Funeral Of A Great Myth" in *Christian Reflections* (Grand Rapids: Eerdmans, 1967), 88.

18 Stanley Jaki, *The Road of Science and the Ways To God* (Chicago: University of Chicago, 1978), 280.

an evolutionary ethic. In Huxley's thought, ethical and moral considerations must be intimately connected to the larger nature of reality itself and specifically human nature. *If* evolution is the law of the cosmos, then the interests of logical consistency point in such a direction as he suggests. For this reason, separating the purely scientific aspects of evolutionary theory from the broader doctrines of evolutionism is not as easy as some suggest. Nor have such attempts as Teilhard de Chardin's (*The Phenomenon of Man*) to combine evolutionary thought with Christian theism demonstrated that such reconciliation is possible. Although Dobzhansky saw Teilhard's thought as a "ray of hope," others of a materialist persuasion have tended to dismiss his ideas as naïve, pious nonsense.

It is outside our purposes here to give detailed consideration of the varieties of ways in which Christianity and evolutionism interact in systems of "theistic evolution" or "process" theologies. Suffice it to say here that such visions are attempts on the part of scientists and theologians to create an attractive synthesis between theism and the conclusions of evolutionary science (see Appendix II of this book for a focused consideration of one such approach). It bears noting, however, that such systems are often challenged and even scorned from both theological and scientific perspectives.

Darwin's emergence as a writer in the mid and later nineteenth century had a dual effect on the emergent vision of evolutionism. The philosophic idea of evolutionism, which was itself a quasi-religion in its own right, existed before Darwin's revolutionary writings. As Michael Ruse has shown, "[e]volution had been in the air for a long time, and many people had been looking for a reason to believe it."[19] Ruse sees Darwin's work as giving impetus to, rather than creating a base for, evolutionism. However, the philosophy gathered new fuel and momentum from Darwin and encouraged people to think of the quasi-religion as indistinguishable from "science." Evolutionism became a worldview through which vast multitudes sought to interpret all aspects of experience, a virtual meaning system of compelling power and attraction, "a science-based ideology

---

19   Michael Ruse, *The Evolution-Creation Struggle* (Cambridge, Mass., Harvard University Press, 2005), 85.

that could explain the meaning of life,"[20] making possible what Richard Dawkins famously has called an "intellectually fulfilled atheism." Indeed, from the very beginning evolutionism was posed as an alternative meaning system replacing the traditional, now "superstitious" worldview of Christianity. That it has been unable to do that for great masses of people around the world seems to be an irritant to a more recent and intellectually militant generation of materialist writers in the fashion of Dawkins (e.g. Sam Harris, A.N. Wilson, Christopher Hitchens).

Christianity and Science: The Alleged "Warfare"

These tensions are played out against one of the major myths of modern life, the alleged "warfare" between science and religion ("religion" usually means "Christianity" in this construction). This narrative is usually threaded with specifically anti-Catholic polemics, and rests substantially on the notorious Galileo affair of the seventeenth century. This storyline is typically linked to the 1925 Scopes Trial to prove that religion, specifically Christian faith, is unalterably opposed to scientific inquiry and hence is the enemy of reason, learning, and progress. Great numbers of people take this alleged conflict for granted, and I would guess that they include an overwhelming number of professors in colleges and universities. Further, this notion's uncritical acceptance provides the soil for pop culture products like Dan Brown's *Da Vinci Code* and *Angels and Demons*. This makes it very difficult for the alternative story to be heard. I will seek to summarize a balancing viewpoint here.

Science, as a methodology and an organized, principled activity, emerged within the context of medieval Christian civilization. Indeed, the great mathematician and philosopher Alfred North Whitehead acknowledged that modern science emerged *only* within a context of Christian theism, and did so as its logical and consistent expression. This development was primarily the result of the interaction of Greek thought and the biblical tradition. The biblical view of God as lawgiver and creator was combined with the Greek view of an

---

20   Ibid., 96

orderly and regular cosmos. On this basis it was possible to assume that *nature is knowable.* Also, the Bible takes an affirmative attitude toward the natural world, seeing in it a revelation of God's glory. This theme is sounded in many of the Psalms. Furthermore, God's purpose is being worked out in the created order, and man himself is given dominion over the rest of creation. These insights were understandably friendly to scientific inquiry.

The most important consideration here is the biblical basis for a viable epistemology, especially in view of evolutionism's difficulties in this regard, discussed above. The Christian theologian Francis Schaeffer observed:

> Let me be clear as to why there is no problem of epistemology in the Christian structure. . . . In the area of biblical Christianity, Galileo, Copernicus, Kepler, Francis Bacon—all these men, up to Newton and Faraday—understood that there was a universe there because God had made it. And they believed, as Whitehead has so beautifully said, that because God was a reasonable God one could discover the truth of the universe by reason.[21]

A similar attitude toward the natural world was prevalent in the nineteenth century, in which "many of the leading men of science were men of deep faith, while clergymen and theologians also pursued scientific research."[22] The Protestant Reformation itself had given a specific impetus to science among the Puritans of England. Physicist and theologian Ian Barbour writes that "seventeenth-century England was the turning point in the history of science . . . and the Puritans were its chief agents."[23] We may acknowledge, then, that biblical ideas have made a real contribution to the development

---

21 Francis Schaeffer, *He is There and He is Not Silent* (Wheaton,Ill., Tyndale House, 1972), 67.

22 Evan Marie Garroutte, "The Positivist Attack on Baconian Science and Religious Knowledge in the 1870s" in Christian Smith, ed., *The Secular Revolution* (Berkeley, University of California Press, 2003), 197

23 Barbour, *Issues in Religion and Science,* 48.

of science by providing a workable framework of presuppositions upon which scientific inquiry could build.

The "Protestant ethic" also played a role. One of the reasons cited by Barbour for this contribution was the Calvinist emphasis on the integrity and value of "worldly" work. That is, Calvinists rejected the idea that specifically religious vocations were superior to "secular" ones. A person could serve God through honest and useful labor on the grounds that it was fascinating in itself, beneficial to mankind, and divinely sanctioned. "It thus appears that both the biblical doctrine of creation and the vocational ethic of Puritanism contributed positively to the rise of science."[24] Indeed, one of the great masterpieces of art to come out of Calvinist Holland effectively symbolizing this is Jan Vermeer's painting *The Astronomer*, which shows the scientist bathed in luminous light as he hovers over his work.

Isaac Newton himself—sometimes judged to be the greatest scientist who ever lived—offers a most interesting case of connectedness between a theological outlook and scientific inquiry. A number of claims are made about Newton today to explain away his known expressions of theism. Some allege that he didn't mean what he said. Rather, he was just engaging in a "cover" maneuver to keep the nefarious, heresy-hunting church at bay. Or, his writings on theology and biblical prophecy, which indicate belief in a God who acts in the affairs of humanity, can be attributed to mental confusion born of old age.

Newton's theological views were clearly unorthodox. Be that as it may, it seems clear today that he was certainly no atheist, and viewed the universe as an intelligently, rationally ordered whole. His writings on theology and biblical studies eventually came to light in the early twentieth century when the world-famous economist John Maynard Keynes purchased them. Keynes, who was a Newton enthusiast and collector, judged that the scientist's writings revealed

---

24 Ibid., 50.

a belief in "the universe as a cryptogram set by the Almighty."[25] If Keynes was correct in this assessment, then we might well conclude that Isaac Newton was a believer in intelligent design in nature. Students of today, who may encounter ridicule for any positive curiosity about the contemporary Intelligent Design movement, may be interested to know that Isaac Newton was, apparently, a kindred spirit.

In view of this background, one wonders how modern man came to the point of seeing Christian faith and science as being in conflict, with some scientists claiming to deal with "facts" as opposed to "superstition." Considering this question calls attention to the general tendency toward secularism growing out of the European "Enlightenment," an epoch that shaped the modern world in fundamental ways. Modernity, like religious faith, is characterized by certain assumptions—or presuppositions—that guide its conclusions. However factual and objective materialists may claim to be in contrast to "the superstitions of religion," they also are guided by certain assumptions that are taken on faith. The question for our understanding is whether the "facts" of modern thought are the necessary recognition of evidences or the necessary conclusions growing out of a set of assumptions taken on faith.

The triumph of science and its alleged power to address all issues of human life is expressed in words engraved in the frieze of the Smithsonian Institute's Museum of Technology in Washington, D.C. The statement abstracts the essence of a worldview embraced by the major promoters of Darwinist evolutionism: "Science is the pursuit above all which impresses us with the capacity of man for intellectual and moral progress and awakens the human intellect to aspiration for a higher condition of humanity." This statement by James Smithson is the result of a long development and revolution in thought that we must understand in order to grasp the nature of the "creation-evolution" controversy.

---

25 The story of Newton's "lost" letters and manuscripts of theology is vividly summarized by Rodney Stark, *For the Glory of God* (Princeton, N.J.: Princeton University Press, 2003), 167-172.

The Enlightenment, or "Age of Reason," is sometimes given a convenient birth-date of 1687, the year that saw the publication of Newton's *Mathematical Principles of Natural Philosophy*. This era, which comprised the eighteenth century, witnessed the formation of a worldview that continued to have a powerful impact through the nineteenth century and into our own time. We remain under the influence of the philosophic assumptions of the Enlightenment to an extraordinary degree. The Enlightenment mentality was characterized by a profound confidence in the powers of human reason, derived in part from the earlier discoveries of Copernicus and Galileo in the area of astronomy, as well as Newton's work relative to the laws of motion and gravity. The work of these men had come to fruition through the powers of observation and abstract reasoning. Further, the eighteenth century saw a rising tide of confidence that these processes of discovering truth were adequate to arrive at a comprehensive view of the world. Nature came to be viewed as a self-sustaining mechanism that could be explained entirely in terms of "natural law."

The dominant conception of God was that of *Deism*, in which the deity was understood to have set natural laws in place while keeping any further personal, revelatory activity separated and remote from human affairs. As this view of divine presence took hold, it became increasingly apparent that such a remote God was not really all that different from an altogether absent deity. Deism, in this sense, represented a certain presupposition about God that led easily and logically to atheism itself. Inasmuch as the deist "god" did not reveal itself in any personal way to the world, the concept of divine revelation was increasingly viewed as irrelevant, arbitrary, and superstitious. The discovery of truth, if possible at all, would be carried forth solely through the given powers of reason.

This total confidence in reason had momentous consequences for the general understanding of life and historical Christian belief. One of the more important developments was a widespread skepticism toward ancient and medieval documents upon which much pre-Enlightenment knowledge was based. Numerous documents formerly trusted were shown to be spurious, with skepticism logically extended toward the Bible as well. The effect upon Christianity was to fuel a mounting attack upon the church's foundations—whether Protestant or Catholic—and encouraging skepticism toward the historically dominant Christian worldview among philosophers, intellectuals, educators, scholars, and even theologians.

The general skepticism served to break down Christian meaning structures in the following significant ways:

1.) The Bible, once trusted, was considered by scholars to be in error unless proved correct by archaeological or documentary evidence. If disparities existed between biblical statements and other sources, the Bible was held to be suspect. The "higher criticism" of biblical scholars attempted to understand the biblical literature on a purely naturalistic presuppositional base, which itself guided them to skeptical conclusions concerning the historicity and integrity of the Scriptures.

2.) The confidence in reason, philosophy, and science militated against belief in the "supernatural." As a result, the miraculous content of the Scriptures was regarded as imaginary and fabulous. The classic example of this is David Strauss's view, expressed in his classic *Life of Jesus,* that all accounts of the miraculous or encounters with the "supernatural" were to be automatically attributed to "mythical" elements added to an original historical core. These assumptions still guide the orthodox approach to biblical studies in most college and university programs. Traditional evidences cited for the Bible's inspiration were explained away, most notably the premise of predictive prophecy. All such evidence was dismissed as *vaticinium ex eventu,* or things written *after* their seeming fulfillment. This view, which is grounded in presuppositions against the very possibility of predictive prophecy, is widely held today among the theologically "liberal" elements in today's Christendom.

3.) Christian faith was forced to reinterpret its historic teachings to accommodate the Enlightenment worldview. The concepts of sin and redemption gave way to beliefs in the basic goodness and perfectibility of human life. The doctrine of God's *grace* (unmerited favor) came to be overshadowed by an emphasis on human works as a means of salvation. Salvation itself came to be understood in terms of an imagined utopian future to be brought about through the application of human science to individual and social issues, as suggested in the Smithsonian quote above.

Thus, Enlightenment thought embraced a radical "anti-supernaturalism." Perhaps this is an insufficient and overly negative way of stating it. Nevertheless, I think it is a valid characterization and of some value. For, as a result of the rationalism of the age, all reality was now to be interpreted in accordance with purely naturalistic premises. This mode of thought eventually extended to the consideration of life's beginnings and human destiny.

> So impressive were the achievements of science that men were stimulated to apply the analytical methods of science to social problems. A great search took place for natural laws which would help explain all phenomena. Natural laws of politics, economics, and even religion, it was thought, might be discovered in much the same way that Galileo and Newton had found the laws of motion and gravitation. This essentially hopeful viewpoint gradually evolved into a belief in progress.[26]

Recent historical scholarship reveals the essentially polemical, anti-historical character of the so-called "war" between Christianity and science. Writers like Stanley Jaki and Rodney Stark, among a good number of others, have addressed this accusation and found it be essentially false. Jaki explores the intriguing question as to why science, as an ongoing method of inquiry, began and grew in the intellectual/ spiritual soil of medieval Christianity in contrast to its "stillbirth" in other great cultures of the past.[27] Stark, the leading sociologist of religion in America, writes of "the traditional relationship between theology and science" which, he affirms, is being re-asserted by an increasing number of writers who are trained in both theology and scientific disciplines (e.g. Ian Barbour, Paul Davies, John Polkinghorne).

---

26 Richard M. Brace, *The Making of The Modern World* (New York: Holt, Rinehart and Winston, 2nd edition, 1961), 357.

27 See Stanley L. Jaki, *The Savior of Science* (Washington, D.C.: Regnery Gateway, 1988)

In his masterful historical study *For The Glory of God,* Stark makes the essential point that science arose "only once in history—in medieval Europe," and that "science could only arise in a culture dominated by belief in a conscious, rational, all-powerful Creator" who had created nature according to rational laws that could be discerned by reasoning creatures. Stark cites Nobel laureate in physics Charles Townes' efforts to demonstrate that God is a necessary element in any comprehensive explanation of the universe, pointing out that *such efforts are in keeping with a long tradition* that became severed only with the advent of Darwinism. Stark provides a list of 52 scientists who contributed important work to the modern scientific tradition, indicating that fifty were either conventionally "religious" or actually "devout." Fifteen were ecclesiastical figures (priests, monks, ministers, etc.). This would mean nothing other than that many of the developers of modern, scientific knowledge embraced the recognition of a divine intelligence at work in nature.[28]

Indeed, the much-ballyhooed conflict between science and religion is largely the result of nineteenth-century polemics issued in the interests of creating a secular social order. Christian Smith, of the University of North Carolina at Chapel Hill, attributes this myth-building to the emergence of the soft science of sociology and the desire of its leaders to establish purely secular foundations for modern higher education. According to Smith, himself a sociologist, "the historical secularization of American higher education—and of American public life more generally—was not an abstract, natural, and inevitable by-product of some evolutionary modernization process. Rather it was the achievement of intentional agents, influenced by particular ideologies and interests, seeking to enhance their own status and authority by actively displacing the competing status and authority of religious actors."[29]

---

28   Rodney Stark, *For The Glory of God,* 197. See also Stark's broader discussion, 121-199.

29   Christian Smith, editor, *The Secular Revolution: Power, Interests, and Conflict in the Secularization of American Public Life* (Berkeley: University of California Press, 2003),105.

One of the writers in Smith's edited collection of essays (*The Secular Revolution*), Eva Marie Garroutte, indicates that a large share of the so-called "warfare" between science and Christianity was simply made up as a strategy devised in the interests of intellectual hegemony. Secularists, inspired by evolutionism and its collection of ideas derived from the writings of Herbert Spencer, Darwin, and T.H. Huxley, did not like the fact that religious leaders were so involved in scientific research and wanted to strip their voices of any impact or authority. Scientific people desired "exclusive authority" in discussions of science. "The motivation for the anti-religious attack of the 1870s is apparent. One of the central requirements of professionalization is that a group of actors must succeed in drawing clear boundaries between those who have the authority to speak on a certain subject and those who do not." These "actors" sought a situation "in which they could speak about any subject and draw any conclusion, without challenges based on religious values."[30] That they succeeded is readily apparent in modern education and intellectual life in general. Who is "qualified" to speak with authority concerning human nature, the origin of life, and the meaning of the phenomenal world? Always, priority is given to the scientist, with philosophers, theologians, and artists regarded as questionable intruders into the conversation.

Both Rodney Stark and Christian Smith cite Andrew Dickson White's classic of 1896, *A History of the Warfare of Science with Theology in Christendom,* as exemplifying these larger trends. Although his book is no longer taken seriously by professional intellectual historians and historians of science, White's anti-Christian polemics had a deep impact on popular perception of Christianity's relationship to science. Again we might note novelist Dan Brown, who still draws upon White's mythologies and introduces his inaccurate assessments into the popular culture of our day.

Given this context, we may understand how agnosticism and atheism came to be connected with an "intellectually sophisticated" view of life. Also, given the confidence in human capacities for improvement or even human perfection through progress, we can

---

30 Ibid., 200-201

understand how various historic evolutionary philosophies gradually gained favor among intellectuals and eventually the popular imagination.

As evolutionary concepts combined with the rationalistic humanism of the Enlightenment, the modern conflicts between science and historic Christianity began to unfold. This controversy is necessitated wherever evolutionary materialism is elevated to the status of a metaphysical system capable of explaining and integrating the various dimensions of human existence. These considerations return us to the central thread of our discussion, which will now focus upon aspects of *myth*, as applied to evolutionism. The question we pose focuses on whether the evolutionary view of life, as proposed by its most ardent promoters, is *necessitated by evidence* as the inevitable conclusion of any normal, intelligent person, or whether it express aspects of pre-scientific myth and philosophy.

Evolutionism and myth

C.S. Lewis, whose professional life was engaged in the understanding of myths, cited evolution as a celebrated romantic myth long before Darwin's *Origin of Species* appeared in 1859. Although Lewis carefully distinguished between evolution as a scientific hypothesis and an overall mythical vision, he suggests that evolutionary science emerged in the imagination of the West that had been made ready to receive it. "The prophetic soul of the big world was pregnant with the Myth: if science had not met the imaginative need, science would not have been so popular. But probably every age gets, within certain limits, the science it desires."[31]

According to Lewis, popular evolutionary thought conjured up a picture of things moving ever onward and upward. Before a real scientific theory of evolution had been developed, the mythical imagination was looking for a substantiation of this vision—a point made similarly by Michael Ruse, previously cited. The emerging science satisfied this demand. Evolutionists will naturally find this analysis irritating and prejudicial, especially in view of Lewis's

---

31   Lewis, *Christian Reflections*, 84-85

well-known role as Christian apologist. Nevertheless, others have made similar observations. Historian Harry Elmer Barnes, who was certainly no apologist for Christianity, likewise distinguished between the general philosophical conception of naturalistic development and the more precise and restricted field of biological investigation, stating that Darwin "vindicated" evolutionary doctrine.[32]

The philosophical conception of evolution has a long and interesting history. There is nothing peculiarly new about the idea, except for its attachment to the modern idea of progress and its obviously powerful, monopolistic impact on the practice of science. The ancient Greek philosophers Empedocles, Heraclitus, and Anaxagoras first propounded evolutionary teachings, and Aristotle contributed to evolutionary speculation in his idea of a continuous gradation of living entities culminating in man. The Roman poet and philosopher Lucretius, in his work *On The Nature of Things,* applied a concept of evolution to the development of the universe as well as human society and culture. (I can remember being mildly surprised, upon reading Lucretius in a college humanities course, at how "Darwinian" his ancient writings seemed.)

In the eighteenth and nineteenth centuries, evolutionary thinking gained prominence through the efforts of numerous men who prepared the foundations for Darwinism. Charles Darwin's grandfather, Erasmus Darwin, anticipated the ideas of his grandson by decades. The struggle for existence was defined in the work of T.R. Malthus. Other important contributions were made by the Frenchman Jean Lamark (1744-1829), the Englishman Sir Charles Lyell (1797-1875), and the German philosopher Georg Hegel (1780-1831).

Lamark introduced the idea that acquired characteristics in animals could be passed on to succeeding generations. The most familiar illustration of this thought is the story of how the giraffes developed long necks. Supposedly giraffes had to stretch their necks to reach higher leaves and branches, passing on to offspring an increased neck length. Not surprisingly, Lamark's views have been

---

32 Harry Elmer Barnes, *An Intellectual and Cultural History of the Western World,* 3 vol. (New York: Dover Publications, 1965), 3: 958-960

largely discredited in contemporary evolutionary thinking, although they showed up in some science instruction that I experienced in elementary school in the 1950s.

Lyell's contribution was to posit the principle of *uniformitarianism,* which proposed to explain the past history of the earth in terms of presently observed processes. This principle was initially applied to the discipline of geology, and is stated in the title of Lyell's major work—*Principles of Geology, Being an Attempt to Explain the Former Changes of the Earth's Surface, by Reference to Causes Now in Operation.* A modern textbook, in presenting this principle, states that "the external and internal processes we recognize today have been operating unchanged, and at the same set of rates, throughout most of Earth's history."[33] Lyell's formulation contradicted the alternative premise of *catastrophism,* which assumed a series of cataclysmic events in the earth's past. This latter view was favored by a significant number of Christians who sought to reconcile the biblical account of the Noahic flood with geological science. Lyell's principle was adopted by most geologists. Catastrophism seemed too unpredictable a principle upon which to base geological science, and uniformitarianism was more convenient to the naturalistic and anti-biblical mentality fostered by the Enlightenment. However, Lyell's principle was attractive to many Christians as well, who reasoned that it supported a lawful God in a lawful universe.[34]

We should note the fact that uniformitarianism did not constitute a "discovery" as such. Rather, it was the statement of a basic assumption upon which the science of geology would develop. Its basic influence was twofold. Biblically, it militated against the acceptance of the Genesis flood as a real event. It also provided a basis for interpreting fossil deposits in terms of an evolutionary sequence over vast periods of time.

---

33 Richard F. Flint and Brian J. Skinner, *Physical Geology* (New York: John Wiley and Sons, 1974), 19.

34 An interesting account of the "catastrophist-uniformitarian controversy" is given in Charles C. Gillispie, *Genesis and Geology* (New York: Harper Torchbooks, 1951).

In Germany, George Hegel utilized evolutionary concepts in his metaphysical system. Hegel's vision held that all progress and development was caused by confrontations of events or ideas constituting a pattern of *thesis* and *antithesis*. Out of this confrontation comes, in Hegel's vision, *synthesis*. Hegel's ideas came to exert a remarkable influence on the subsequent history of socioeconomic theory, particularly Marxism, and some philosophers used his ideas to support Darwinism.

It is apparent, then, that evolutionism was in the air, but the ideas set forth by Charles Darwin did not actually initiate, through compelling evidences, belief in evolution. Rather, his work fed into a stream of speculative philosophy that had existed for centuries and which was given increasing plausibility as it merged with the naturalistic presuppositions of the Enlightenment.

Ian Barbour, in his work *Myths, Models, and Paradigms,* discusses five basic characteristics of *myth*.[35]

1. Myths define ways of ordering experience. They provide a worldview and overall vision of reality. Also, myths are set in primordial time, at creation.
2. Myths inform human life concerning self-identity and ancestry.
3. Myths express a saving power in human life. That is, the vision contains an ideal state or being which represents the source, ground, and goal of all life. The actual condition of humanity is separated from the ideal by some flaw or defect requiring healing through a savior or discipline to be followed.
4. Myths provide patterns for human action.
5. Myths are enacted in rituals and symbols.

These qualities are, of course, readily applicable to Christian faith and religion in general. Barbour finds them also applicable to evolutionism and scientific materialism.

---

35 Ian G. Barbour, *Myths, Models, and Paradigms,* (New York: Harper and Row, 1974), 20-21.

The broad definition would include modern secular philosophies whose stories, while not about the gods, do deal with "aspects of the cosmic order." Marxism and evolutionary naturalism are world-visions with most of the characteristics described above. Some authors speak of modern "covert myths" of inevitable progress, human rationality, and utopia through technology.[36]

In other words, evolutionism has many characteristics of religious mythology, the implications of which are set forth by one of the myth's foremost evangelists, George G. Simpson.

As applied to mankind, that [evolutionary] interpretation shows that we did not appear all at once but by an almost incredibly long and slow progression. It shows too that there was no anticipation of man's coming. He responds to no plan and fulfills no supernal purpose. He stands alone in the universe, a unique product of a long, unconscious, impersonal, material process, with unique understandings and potentialities. These he owes to no one but himself, and it is to himself that he is responsible. . . . He can and must decide and manage his own destiny."[37]

In this vision, we find elements of a heroic view of life along with aspects of cosmic mystery. Humanity owes no allegiance to a creator, and human life is without meaning other than what individuals can carve out for themselves. In contrast to the Christian concept of the "Fall," and in a kind of negative symmetry to it, the human race is risen out of an improbable process that did not even desire its presence in nature. Humanity has overcome time, chance, and

---

36 Ibid.
37 quoted by Bolton Davidheiser, *Evolution and Christian Faith* (Presbyterian and Reformed Publishing Company, 1968), 149.

improbability to stand, collectively, as a solitary Titan constructing, rather than meeting, Destiny.

This myth has aspects of tragedy as well, illustrated in the contemplations of mathematician and philosopher Bertrand Russell, that "all the labor of the ages, all the devotion; all the inspiration; all the noonday brightness of human genius are destined to extinction in the vast death of the solar system, and . . . the whole temple of Man's achievement must inevitably be buried beneath the debris of a universe in ruins."[38]

Christians are in error, I believe, in characterizing this way of thinking as denigrating to man. If it were so, it is doubtful that the myth could sustain itself for very long. But as we have seen, it has been around for a long time and has gained extraordinary power over the past century. There is power in the myth, and "grandeur" as Darwin himself recognized. It offers the attraction of autonomy, freedom, and the imperative of courage. There is something awesome, enigmatic, and beautiful in the contemplation of the all-so-improbable spark of life in the primordial silence, and its ascent, age upon age, to the consciousness of its own transience. In its way, this scenario has a visionary power for the materialist that the Christian finds in the mystery of Christ's resurrection. The expression of this myth found a dramatic interpretation in American popular culture in the Disney classic *Fantasia*. Even works of art created within a Christian and biblical cultural context are claimed for evolutionism, as seen in Theodosius Dobzhansky's interpretation of Michelangelo's *Creation of Adam* on the Sistine Ceiling as a "symbolic representation of Creation by evolution."[39]

Having come this far, we may better understand the nature of Paul B. Sears's ardent rapture toward the central hero of the myth:

> The best we can hope to do is to examine ourselves,
> and try to see wherein our behavior and our modes

---

38   Bertrand Russell, *Mysticism and Logic and Other Essays* (New York: Norton, 1929), cited by Richard H. Bube, *The Human Quest* (Waco, Tex.: Word, 1971), 157.

39   Dobzhansky, *Evolution, Genetics, and Man*, 374

of thinking, our values, and our sanctions, reflect
the point of view which Darwin represents.[40]

Here we can clearly see that evolutionary naturalism becomes
much more than a biological model for understanding the structural
relationship between living things. It becomes, in fact, a vast, all-
embracing *meaning system* touching upon ultimate issues of life. In
Sears' view, Darwin's thought seems to take on an almost scriptural
authority. A more recent voice in the conversation, Michael
Ruse, a committed evolutionist and professor from Florida State,
acknowledges the way in which evolutionism goes beyond science:

> Evolution is promoted by its practitioners as more
> than mere science. Evolution is promulgated as
> an ideology, a secular religion—a full-fledged
> alternative to Christianity, with meaning and
> morality. . . . Evolution is a religion. This was true
> of evolution in the beginning, and it is true of
> evolution still today.[41]

Darwin, indeed, has become the Presence permeating modern
thought. Inasmuch as the worldview of evolutionism has been
promulgated as the *necessary way of thinking for intelligent people,* in
the name of science, the question now arises: Really?

---

40 Paul B. Sears, *Charles Darwin* (New York: Charles Scribner's Sons, 1950), 2.
41 Michael Ruse, "Saving Darwinism from the Darwinians," *National Post*
(May 13, 2000), B-3.

Part II

Compelling Belief?

"Evolution has an impact on every aspect of man's thinking: his philosophy, his metaphysics, his ethics."
—Ernst Mayr (interview with *Omni* magazine, February, 1983)

The most avid promoters of a purely naturalistic (i.e. materialistic) worldview hold that the evidence *compels* any thoughtful, modern, intellectually honest person to embrace or "make peace" with an atheism rooted in evolution. Current voices along these lines are led by the Oxford zoologist Richard Dawkins, who more-or-less recapitulates the conclusions of earlier figures like G.G. Simpson, Bertrand Russell, Julian Huxley, and the French biologist Jacques Monod. Dawkins is joined by A.N. Wilson, William Provine, the less-polemical Stephen Hawking and other voices in academic circles.

That the evidence does *not* compel any such thing is demonstrated by the number of perfectly competent scientists who, while carrying out their scientific work, embrace at least some generalized form of theistic belief. Others actually participate enthusiastically in Christian churches and may be counted as firm believers in the gospel of Christ. One may notice, too, an increasing number of books located in the "Science" sections of bookstores that feature authors who write positively concerning the sciences and theism from the perspective of people trained in scientific disciplines (e.g. Francis Collins, John Polkinghorne, Gerald Schroeder, Frank J. Tipler). This development might indicate that the dichotomy drawn by Richard Dawkins and similar writers is perhaps strained beyond what actual evidence suggests, leading ardent materialists to the last refuge of authoritarianism—*ad hominem* attacks on such people as cowardly, deluded, or weak-minded compromisers.[42] Yet, we can pose an important question here. *If* the evidences are so overwhelming for nature's "go-it-alone" bootstraps development, why should there be any scientists at all who embrace *any* sort of theism? Can we really believe that all such people, with credible scientific degrees and research results to their credit, are merely weak-minded anti-intellectuals clinging to childish beliefs?

Another question pertains to the existence of societies of scientists who affirm science, including evolution, along with theistic belief. Why do such organizations (for example the Discovery Institute)

---

42 For a particularly acidic example of this approach see Richard Dawkins, *The God Delusion* (Boston: Houghton Mifflin, 2008).

exist at all? How did they come into existence, and why? Indeed, it is clear that such groups did not form out of thin air to challenge evolutionary teaching, but formed because enough scientists and philosophers of science were seeing something that gave them pause concerning the standard Darwinian narrative. What did they see?

Darwinism: Why any questions at all?

This section will attempt to present some of the major lines of argument that pose questions concerning Darwinism. Before proceeding, however, it is worth noting that on the average college campus of our day it is almost impossible to approach this subject without stirring up emotions. I well remember a meeting of some faculty who had been called together to see if a public dialogue might be possible, and the tension in the room where we met was so thick that the colleague who had initiated the idea quickly e-mailed us all announcing he was calling it off in the interests of collegial harmony.

This kind of situation is stirred by a couple of fundamental factors. On the one hand, some very noisy opponents of evolution from the religious communities tend to go beyond reasoned critique into patterns of indictment, often of the most extreme and insulting character. Evolutionists are blinded, deceived by the Devil, or are regarded as agents of antichrist. Interestingly enough, this line of attack actually strengthens the stereotype that all opposition to Darwinism is fueled by little more than religion and accusation. On the other hand, evolutionists might tend toward a mentality that asks: "Why should I be bothered with this?" They may be inclined to dismiss arguments questioning Darwinism that come from scientific thinking as little more than "religion in disguise," thereby deflecting any need to consider or respond to reasonable questions.

I believe the line of questioning represented in what follows is reasonable, and will show that the claims made on behalf of a *necessary* link between evolutionary science and hard naturalism is overrated, and that intelligent individuals may proceed to explore the "God question" without first genuflecting in the direction of Charles

Darwin, and that students are wrong to think that scientific pursuit requires of them a rejection of theistic belief.

Our task here is to call into question the alleged persuasiveness of evolutionism as a necessary way for intelligent people to think, for it is in the name of this view of things that the traditional theistic meaning systems are declared invalid. I believe that the world is created, and I see good reason to believe that and consider the implications. If someone tells me that my persuasion is invalid, irrational, or just plain stupid on the basis of evidence to the contrary, then I'll want to inquire to see if those evidences are really as weighty and as infallible as proposed.

Statements of immense confidence in the atheistic implications of evolution emerged in the later nineteenth century, most notably from the statements of the German biologist Ernst Haeckel. Haeckel popularized the notion that all the rich variety of life on this planet owed its origin to a single primordial source from which it developed, from "lower" and simpler forms to "higher" and more complex forms guided by what the Darwinians call "natural selection." Gradually, first in the intellectual classes and then more broadly in the laity, the general conviction grew that divine action in creation was no longer a reasonable idea. Haeckel declared: "The mystery of the universe is explained, the Deity annulled, and a new era of infinite knowledge [has been] ushered in."[43] Today these words sound like sophomoric pretention. Yet, they played a role in shaping a general consciousness that scientific evidences were inexorably in conflict with theistic assumptions about the origin and the *purpose* of life. The philosophical and *religious* extent of evolutionary thought touched upon everything. The grand reach of evolution-as-evolution*ism* is expressed by moral philosopher Mary Midgley:

> Evolution is the creation-myth of our age. By telling us our origins it shapes our views of what we are. It influences not just our thought, but our feelings and actions, too, in a way which goes far beyond its official function as a biological theory.

---

43 Cited by Ian Barbour, *Issues In Science and Religion,* 109.

> In calling it a myth, I am not of course saying that
> it is a false story. I mean that it has great symbolic
> power, which is independent of its truth. Is the word
> religion appropriate to it?[44]

These are impressive claims, to be sure, and are empowered by
the status and prestige accorded science in the modern world. They
directly put the God of Christian theism "in the dock" for evaluation
and judgment. Although they were set forth many decades ago,
and have been much critiqued through the years, they are finding
renewed life in the popular writings of Richard Dawkins and others
who seek to convince us that atheism is, in fact, the only intelligent
position one can take in the face of scientific advance. These claims
call for thoughtful response on the part of Christians who find it
unacceptable that a dichotomy should be posited between faith and
reason, devotion and learning. What should a Christian response
be?

A Christian response is twofold. First, the Christian must bring
forth positive evidence in support of the truth of Christian faith. It is
not enough to simply denounce evolution and evolutionists, for even
if one were to present a convincing case against Darwinism, that in
itself would mean nothing in respect to the validity or credibility of
the Christian faith. Secondly, the Christian must voice meaningful
criticism toward those systems that deny and ridicule the faith.
Again, our discussion here falls into the second category and seeks
the limited purpose of demonstrating the intellectual difficulties
of evolutionism. In doing this much we may hope to at least erode
some intellectual barriers that prevent people from investigating the
Christian alternative.

The concern for evidence is basic to any meaningful human
dialogue. Without it, matters of truth are left to whim, and too often
what is "true" represents nothing more than a personal preference.
Certain popular forms of "non-doctrinal" Christianity, which
weakly state that "it means different things to different people,"

---

44 Mary Midgley, "The Religion of Evolution" in John Durant, ed., *Darwin and Divinity*, 154.

are rightly shunned by thinking people. If it is *that* kind of faith that the materialist rejects, we must point out that it is also rejected by millions of Christians as well. It is founded on little more than sentiment and emotional disposition, an easy contrast to the "hard and objective thought" alleged to be the contrasting province of science. Insofar as evidence enters into the realms of science and religion, it is broadly assumed that evidence is pertinent and possible only in the former realm but is irrelevant to the latter. Science is "factual" and "objective" whereas religious faith is arbitrary and "dogmatic," sentimental, emotional, and anti-intellectual.

One of the more interesting observations to be made in this regard is that science is considerably less objective than is widely thought. Conversely, it may be shown that Christian faith is considerably more objective than generally believed. It is, after all, predicated upon certain historical claims concerning events alleged to have taken place in a specific cultural context and a specific time in history. It can, therefore, be subjected to investigation. Science, like religious faith, rests on certain assumptions—concepts posited as starting points and accepted as axiomatic before evidence plays a meaningful role. God's creation of the world is an assumed starting point, not the result of any evidence. Similarly, the assertion that the universe has existed eternally and takes the form it does through no will or intention beyond itself is another assumption—that of the materialist/atheist. It also is a statement of faith. My own personal position is that evolution does not weigh necessarily in either direction.

I will seek to show that there is a good deal of subjectivity in the worldview of evolutionism. It is my position that the problems with evolutionism as a worldview are both philosophic and scientific, and that a skeptical Christian can be, at the same time, an intelligent modern person and someone of Christian faith without "sacrificing one's intellect."

Observations and interpretations

Let us initially consider the relationship between observations and *modes of interpretation*. In science, as in religion, a "fact" is quite often determined by the convenience of data to the set of ideas forming the vehicle of interpretation. Both the Christian and the materialist deal with the same data, although they may interpret it differently. For example, a geneticist observing and working with DNA at a place like Andrews University—an institution of the creationist Seventh Day Adventist denomination—deals with the same substance as an atheist colleague doing similar research at any typical secular state university. The Adventist researcher, however, may be impressed with the wonder of God's handiwork as his/her work progresses, whereas the materialist may simply see a natural process arising from chance and natural selection, even an evidence against the reality of God. The point here is simple: the contrasting researchers may work effectively with the object of study while coming to completely different conclusions as to the overall meaning of it. Their assumptions of what is ultimately true, constituting their faith, lead them in opposite directions. All scientists, whatever their metaphysical persuasions, deal with the same chemicals, the same processes, the same bones and the same rocks. The raw data is the same for the Christian "creationist" as for the non-theist. Only the interpretation models differ, and that difference will constitute what is accepted as "fact."

Problems arise when data are discovered that defy the interpretive system or when vital evidence that would support a theory is missing. For the average layperson trying to understand the issues, here is where it gets confusing and challenging. Many Christians, for example, don't know how to fit the evidences of prehistoric man—"cavemen"—into their interpretations of the Genesis creation account, while such anthropological evidence is embraced by others as a sure evidence of a purely naturalistic evolution of humanity. In the case of evolution, the lay inquirer will come across diametrically opposite conclusions about the fossil record, even from within the evolutionary camp itself. Creationists like to argue that the fossil record does not, in fact, bear out Darwin's predictions or support slow, incremental evolution of life from a single original source. They get quite a bit of mileage out of quoting evolutionists themselves on this matter. Yet again, other evolutionists will claim the existence of thousands of very clear examples of "transitional" forms and "missing links." The average person is likely to be left wondering what the true story is.

Even if major anomalies should arise, they would not quickly overthrow an entire theoretical program. This reality seems lost on the community of young-earth creationists, who spend much effort trying to find inconsistencies and gaps in evolutionary evidences. While anomalies *do* mean something and "count" for or against an acknowledged "truth," they are not likely to be welcomed or even seen to be significant, however spectacular they may be. I once asked a geologist friend what the effect would be on the science of geology should Noah's Ark be discovered in the upper regions of Mount Ararat. My question was in the context of a discussion of the periodic explorations to find the Ark. His answer was "none." He did not seem to acknowledge the potential significance of evidence of a monstrous aqueous and terrestrial catastrophe for the study of earth history, probably because he could not see outside the box of the conventional uniformitarian paradigm.

A similar issue arose many years ago in regard to prints of an apparently upright, bipedal creature reported in Carboniferous rocks. This was the subject of an article in the eminent journal *Scientific American,* January, 1940. Author Albert Ingalls discussed these footprints and remarked that if man, or even an ape ancestor, existed as far back as the Carboniferous age the whole science of geology would be "completely wrong."[45] Anomalous paleontological and archaeological claims like these exist in some abundance, yet tend to get set on the shelf by scientific orthodoxy to be pursued only by people interested in "alternative history" or "forbidden archaeology," discussed on the radio by program hosts in the mold of Art Bell. There, they are easily dismissed as crank ideas not to be taken seriously. Science is no different from most intellectual disciplines, all of which define a certain orthodoxy that determines not only conclusions but even the questions to be asked (or which are forbidden to be asked).

---

45   Albert Ingalls, "The Carboniferous Mystery," *Scientific American,* January, 1940, CLXII, 14.

Contrary evidence will, though, eventually have its effect. During my years of teaching in the area of cultural history, specifically art history, I was intrigued to realize that many of the civilizations that make up the history of the ancient world were, at one time and until relatively recently, thought to be "mythical." They contributed to the romantic vision of "lost civilizations." Primary examples are the ancient civilizations of Egypt, Mesopotamia, and Crete. Things do change and new knowledge arises. There is no reason to think that this is any less true of our understanding of nature than it is of human activity. Indeed, as I will argue later, recent years have made it increasingly difficult to trust the explanatory power of the traditional Darwinian elements of randomness, chance, and natural selection as offering adequate answers in the human quest to understand natural phenomena. This is most apparent to open-minded individuals responding to new knowledge in the areas of astrophysics, physics, microbiology, and genetics as well as the philosophy of science.

Creationists seem overly zealous in the search for anomalies, and I have personally thought that they would do more good by engaging in positive scientific research on various problems such as cures for various diseases. Anomalies, even spectacular ones, do not by themselves overthrow dominant scientific theories. Science could not proceed if theories had to be thrown out with the appearance of every piece of information that did not "fit." Nevertheless, there has been increased attention over the years to the issue of how theoretical postures influence our notions of "fact." Important studies have been made of this issue, two of which we will consider at this point. In regard to the issue of "objectivity" in science, we call attention to the major classic critiques of Arthur Koestler and Ian G. Barbour.

Scientific "objectivity?"

Koestler's work *The Act of Creation* is a most interesting treatment of the creative process in science and art. Koestler, in discussing the "limits of confirmation" in science, points out the tenuous nature of various scientific "truths." Evidence, observes Koestler, can never actually confirm a theory itself but can only demonstrate that one theory is more true than another. We may interpret this to mean a comparison based on the inclusiveness of a theory. Which theory is able to accommodate most of the known data of reality? The most inclusive theory is likely to be closest to the actual truth. Nevertheless, experimental evidence is likely to be falsely understood even if it works comfortably within the interpretive system. Koestler stresses the tentative character of scientific truth and is rightly critical of the tendency to confer upon science a peculiarly privileged intimacy with truth. He quotes the great philosopher of science Karl Popper:

> The old scientific ideal of...absolutely certain, demonstrable knowledge has proved to be an idol. The demand for scientific objectivity makes it inevitable that every scientific statement must remain *tentative forever.* It may indeed be corroborated, but every corroboration is relative to other statements which, again, are tentative. Only in our subjective experiences of conviction, in our subjective faith, can we be "absolutely certain.[46]

Certainly one would never get this impression from reading the assured statements of the outstanding spokesmen for the evolutionist worldview. Popper's statement can provide valuable perspective in the face of dogmatic attitudes in science.

Similarly, Ian Barbour draws attention to the question of "objectivity" in scientific enterprise. Barbour notes that the popular stereotype of science as consisting of precise and objective observation is more myth than reality.[47] He makes observations about science that challenge the understandings of many average laypeople. For example, he notes that there is not a sharp line of demarcation between "observation" and "theory." There are no "uninterpreted facts." What is taken as "fact" is influenced by the active influence of human imagination in the formation of mental constructs (concepts) that guide interpretation. "In the light of actual scientific work . . . [the] view of objectivity must be modified to allow for *the*

---

46 Quoted in Arthur Koestler, *The Act of Creation* (New York: Macmillan, 1964; Dell paperback edition, 1967), 242

47 Ian G. Barbour, *Issues In Science and Religion,* 138-139.

contribution of the scientist as experimental agent, as creative thinker, and as personal self "[italics in original].[48]

Barbour cites Thomas Kuhn's influential study *The Structure of Scientific Revolutions* as a particularly significant challenge to the notion of scientific objectivity. According to Kuhn, the thought and actions of a scientific community are dominated by that community's *paradigms*. Paradigms are defined as "standard examples of scientific work which embody a set of conceptual, methodological and metaphysical assumptions."[49] Paradigms define a coherent research tradition, and scientific education is an induction into the habits of thought presented by textbooks and an initiation into the practice of established scientists. This leads to the acquisition of a strong system of commitments to particular conceptual, theoretical, and instrumental tools. Paradigms guide the direction of "normal" research that, according to Kuhn, attempts to "force nature into the preformed and relatively inflexible boxes the paradigm supplies."[50]

In other words, there is an "acceptable" way of treating data governed in advance by a framework constituting the rules of the game. Paradigms dominate the operations of normal science, and are highly resistant to change. According to Kuhn's analysis, all genuine *scientific revolutions are actually paradigm shifts*. Scientists resist such revolutions because their thinking has been permeated with previous intellectual commitments.

As Barbour notes, Kuhn came under vigorous criticism. He seemed to be emphasizing a subjective element in scientific work, and in fact he modified his views in the face of this criticism. Nevertheless, what seems to have been sustained in subsequent thought is the recognition that "objectivity" is a somewhat slippery concept, and that all data are "theory-laden." Barbour also points out that comprehensive theories are highly resistant to falsification; nevertheless, direct observation does exert some control over theories.[51]

---

48   Ibid., 176
49   Ian G. Barbour, *Myths, Models, and Paradigms*, 93.
50   Ibid., 104.
51   Ibid., 113-118.

For our purposes here, Barbour makes an important point regarding the catalyzing effect of specifically theistic assumptions upon scientific work. In a discussion of the presuppositions that support the scientific enterprise he notes that scientists are often unaware of the given assumptions that support their work and where those assumptions come from. For example, the scientist has an "ingrained conviction concerning the intelligibility, orderliness, and dependability of the world. He does not ask, 'Does this disease have a cause?': he asks, 'What is the cause of this disease?'—that is, he assumes an answer to the first question without ever asking it, and without any formal premise such as 'Same cause, same effect')." Barbour then calls attention to the biblical doctrine of creation and general biblical attitudes toward nature as having encouraged the growth of science. By contrast, "There would be little support for scientific activity in a culture radically permeated by the outlook of atheistic existentialism—for which the world is an irrational chaos, a meaningless stage for the drama of personal existence."[52]

I would apply this thought to the "God delusion" rhetoric of Richard Dawkins. Had Dawkins' own assumptions guided the formative centuries of western civilization it is unlikely that scientific enterprise would ever have arisen! Ironically, in order for Dawkins to carry on his science he must operate out of assumptions set in place by the very worldview he rejects.

Scientific attachment to doctrine: a notorious example

In some celebrated instances, entrenched conceptual constructions have tended to be protected even in the face of substantial contrary evidence. There is perhaps no greater example of this than the now infamous history of the so-called "Biogenetic Law" and the "scientific" drawings employed to support it. The story is recounted by the late Harvard biologist Stephen Jay Gould in his book *I Have Landed*, from which I have taken the following summarization.

---

52 Barbour, *Issues in Science and Religion*, 181-182.

Long promoted as an evidence of the evolution of various creatures from a common source, the Biogenetic Law proposed that embryos of different vertebrate creatures revealed evolutionary history. The similarity of a human embryo to that of fish, salamanders, chickens, etc. indicated a "recapitulation" of our evolutionary history. Drawings by Ernst Haeckel, the famous late nineteenth-century German Darwinian naturalist and Darwinian propagandist, supported this notion.

Gould writes that Haeckel's drawings were inaccurate to a level that can legitimately be called "fraud," and that the recapitulation theory was jettisoned from serious biology by 1910. Nevertheless, not only did Haeckel's drawings continue to be presented in biology textbooks through most of the twentieth century, the false notion of recapitulation remained deeply embedded in popular imagination through the normal approaches to biology instruction in schools, including college and university courses. Professional biologists and teachers of biology "have the right to be both astonished and ashamed by the century of mindless recycling that has led to the persistence of these drawings in a large number, if not a majority, of modern textbooks!"[53] He writes that the uncritical use of Haeckel's "faked" drawings still persisted in textbooks of biology through the 1990s to the year 2000 (Gould wrote this particular book in 2003).

Creationists jump all over this and have presented it as a major scandal of evolutionary deception.[54] Gould seeks to protect the scientific community from the creationists' criticisms by pointing out that textbook writers are just too generalist in their backgrounds, that they don't understand the specifics of all the sub-disciplines of which they have to write. So, they tend to continue in old ways, copying from former books and continuing to present errors, albeit unintentionally.

This, I must say, seems lame. If Haeckel's falsifications (or "fudging" as it has been expressed in recent textbooks) were known

---

53 Stephen Jay Gould, *I Have Landed: The End of a Beginning In Natural History* (New York, Three Rivers Press, 2003), 307-312.
54 See, for example, Jonathan Wells, *Icons of Evolution* (Washington, D.C.: Regnery, 2000).

in the nineteenth century, and the barrenness of the recapitulation theory was recognized by serious biologists by 1910, how could these ideas have achieved such canonical status in biology instruction over the course of a century, even assuming a "generalist" orientation in textbook writers? Some consideration, I think, must be given to the possibility that this persistence is due to the convenience of the theory and its supporting images to an evolutionism seeking a scientific ground. It was Haeckel, after all, who proclaimed the "annulment" of God by virtue of Darwinian science; the "proof" was embedded in embryology.

But let us assume, just for the sake of argument, that Haeckel's drawings were actually accurate and that various vertebrate embryos did in fact manifest the degree of sameness drawn by Haeckel's imagination. Why would one have to assume, on the basis of this data, a purely naturalistic and evolutionary interpretation? Looking at it from the standpoint of an artist, one might just as well argue for a common template used by a creator in the plan for life, an element of "style" inclusive of many variations expressed from a core concept. Haeckel's embryonic images were conclusive "proof" of evolution because the truth of evolutionary descent from common ancestry had already been assumed. The images fit the paradigm. It does not seem to have mattered, according to Gould, that the whole context surrounding them had been discredited. The paradigm stood.

If we understand this, we can see that the conflict between Christianity and scientific materialism is a confrontation *not* between those who understand nature and those who do not, but it is a confrontation of interpretive concepts. It would therefore seem that the Christian can challenge the materialist on the notion that the latter's view of life is based on objective assessment of observed fact as against the Christian's "subjective faith." Ian Barbour notes that science must involve a skepticism aimed at its own assumptions when he writes:

> No scientific theory can be *verified*. One cannot prove that a theory is true by showing that conclusions deduced from it agree with experiment, since (1) future experiments may conflict with the

theory, and (2) another may be equally compatible with present evidence.[55]

Heresy in science

The second assertion in the above quotation is precisely the position taken by the Creation Research Society in its attempts to have the creation model of origins included in public school presentations. Relative to the science of geology, the creationists assert that the data of geological science can be successfully interpreted according to a *catastrophist* model in contrast to the prevailing *uniformitarian* viewpoint of evolution. What is at issue is not data. Both the creationist and the evolutionist must deal with the same fossil evidence or lack of such, the same rocks and sediment. What is at issue in this particular controversy is the interpretive scheme, the lens through which data are filtered and given meaning.

I am not here attempting to defend creationism and attempts to introduce creationist ideas into science courses in schools. Personally, I oppose such efforts. What does interest me is the way in which the mainstream of academic science has reacted with dogmatic denunciation to the positing of an alternative (catastrophist) interpretive scheme in the study of the earth to the prevailing, accepted scheme (Lyell's uniformitarianism). Traditionally, since Darwin's triumph, catastrophism was opposed because it was thought to be friendly to a biblical worldview and its narrative of the great flood of Noah's day. Yet one is puzzled to know why a catastrophist interpretation of the earth's past could not be theologically neutral.

A classic case of scientific outrage over a radical challenge to a prevailing paradigm is the well-known and notorious "Velikovsky Affair" (1950), in which Immanuel Velikovsky offered up a vision of cataclysmic upheavels in the earth's history caused by the near passage to the earth of other celestial bodies. Velikovsky's vision was purely secular. It was not offered in the interests of religion, although he suggested that memories of such catastrophes lived on

---

55   Barbour, *Issues in Science and Religion*, 98.

in the myths of various peoples worldwide. Science professors in American higher education actively sought to suppress his book, even to the point of threatening his publisher, a major publisher of science textbooks. *Newsweek* magazine commented on the situation as follows:

> One of the most cherished rights of the nation's teaching profession is academic freedom, and college professors customarily will fight fiercely to defend it—even at times when it doesn't seem under attack. . . . Although some of the critics who reviewed Velikovsky's book considered it a major scientific contribution, there could be little question but that it had driven the vast majority of the nation's scientists into a highly unacademic frenzy.[56]

Through the ensuing years Velikovsky asked nothing other than to have his ideas considered by the appropriate scientific forums, although he was denied this privilege. Leading the way to ridicule Velikovsky over a period of decades was the Cornell astronomer and popularizer of evolutionism Carl Sagan. Similar ridicule has been more recently heaped upon Lehigh University professor Michael Behe for calling into question the creative capacity of natural selection in such books as *Darwin's Black Box* and *The Edge of Evolution*. Indeed, the mention of Behe's name to academic science professors is likely to stimulate the same irritated and volatile reaction that Velikovsky's did previously.

A challenge to the prevailing paradigms can generate much emotionalism and anger, and there is a real possibility of dogmatism in science that leads to outright suppression of academic freedom. A celebrated case of recent vintage is that of Dean Kenyon, an origin-of-life researcher who, while early in his career had argued for a form of biological determinism asserting that the chemicals that make up life "inevitably" attracted each other. His work in this regard was a focus of critique in A.E. Wilder-Smith's creationist classic *The Creation of*

---

56 See "Professors as Suppressors, *Newsweek*, Vol. XXXVI, No. 1, (July 3, 1950), 15-16.

Life: A Cybernetic Approach to Evolution.[57] Eventually Kenyon came to doubt important premises in contemporary Darwinian thought, and taught some of his criticisms as a professor at San Francisco State University in the 1980s. Interestingly enough, he actually came to gravitate closer to the perspectives of someone like Wilder-Smith, whose critique was grounded in information theory. This exercise in academic freedom earned him a call to appear before academic inquiry hearings and eventually led to his being stripped of his right to teach biology courses.[58] For a layperson like myself, though, I have to ask the question: why did a leading origin-of-life researcher— prominent among materialist scientists—become more aligned in his ideas with a leading Darwinian skeptic/creationist like A.E. Wilder-Smith and the focus of a modern inquisition? I'm curious. What did he see that changed his views? Did he all of a sudden become irrational, superstitious, or intellectually dishonest?

More recently, we have seen the case of an editor at the Smithsonian Institute being disciplined and investigated for publishing a peer-reviewed article by cell biologist Stephen Meyer. Meyer argued for the possibility of intelligent design in the systems of nature. His article, entitled "The Origin of Biological Information in the Higher Taxonomic Categories" argued that no current materialist theory of evolution can account for the appearance of novel animal forms. Meyer's article was fully vetted in the peer-review process, but it was an apparent heresy and proved dangerous for the publication's editor, Dr. Richard Sternberg. Sternberg was vigorously disciplined. He not only lost his office space, but museum administrators interrogated his colleagues concerning his religious and political beliefs.[59]

Breaking from the dominant paradigm is never easy and may lead to marginalization or outright scorn and denunciation. One

---

57   A.E. Wilder-Smith, *The Creation of Life: A Cybernetic Approach to Evolution* (Wheaton, Ill.: Harold Shaw, 1970).

58   Larry Witham, *By Design* (San Francisco, Encounter Books, 2003), 118. This book sets this case, and many others of interest, within the overall context of conflicts arising in recent decades over the scientific objections to Darwinian orthodoxies.

59   See Stephen C. Myer, *Signature in the Cell* (New York: HarperCollins, 2009), 2-3.

cannot help noticing the irony of modern scientists, ever willing to condemn events in history where scientists were ostracized by the church (Galileo is the inevitable example) playing the same role of inquisitors in modern times.

If it is true, though, that paradigms are highly resistant to change, and can even pre-judge contrary evidences, how do changes take place at all?

Clearly, observations do eventually exercise influence. If serious anomalies continue to accumulate, producing a significant degree of discordant data, a new context of understanding will be sought and an alternative theory will emerge. This is seen vividly in the progress from Newtonian to quantum physics. Paradoxically, a shift of paradigms can only occur if, in fact, the previous commitments have been strong. Ian Barbour points out that only a certain tenacity in research programmes can prove scientifically fruitful, for only "if scientists stick with a programme and do not abandon it too readily will its potentialities be systematically explored and exploited."[60] It should not be the case, then, that Darwinians would just role over at the appearance of various challenges to their authority. Conversely, the average layperson interested in these issues is rightly intrigued when a British biochemist, Michael Denton, authors a book with the striking title *Darwinism: A Theory in Crisis*. Intellectually curious people will most likely be intrigued, especially when the professional risks to the author are taken into consideration.

Presuppositions or conclusions?

For over a century Darwinian concepts of life's origin and development have dominated scientific inquiry. Adequate time has been given to the exploration of this theoretical structure, so it is significant to see the growing uneasiness about its reliability among practicing scientists. Whereas laypeople are often given the impression that controversy about Darwinism was settled for intelligent, thinking people in 1925 at the Scopes Trial, this does not seem to be the case at all. Inasmuch as Darwinism has done more

---

60 Barbour, *Myths, Models, and Paradigms*, 114.

than any other system of thought to erode the spiritual authority of Christianity in modern times, a growing recognition of difficulties in the Darwinian picture has important implications for individual thought and society in general.

Darwinians insist that evolution is a *fact*, extrapolating the large, general theory of macroevolution from observed, microevolutionary change. On this basis they recommend evolutionism as a totalistic worldview capable of addressing the human search for meaning (see Part I). However, not all evolutionists are as certain of this as the classic proponents of evolutionary "meaning" have been. One such voice was that of Dr. G.A. Kerkut of Southhampton University, who taught in the department of Physiology and Biochemistry there. His book *Implications of Evolution* (1960) offered up a thoughtful critique that anticipates the later and on-going developments of the later twentieth century. Although an evolutionist himself, Kerkut admits that most books on evolution fail to treat adequately the assumptions upon which the theory rests. "We can believe that such an evolutionary system has taken place, but I for one do not think that 'it has been proved beyond all reasonable doubt.' "[61]

Kerkut did not radically challenge evolutionary thinking. His ideas are very much within an acceptable range of orthodoxy. His book does, however, challenge the Darwinian doctrine that all living things evolved from a unique source, an idea that he held to be *inadequately supported by available evidence.* He also addressed the problem of dogmatism in scientific education, comparing the modern science student to the theology student of the past, accepting ideas on the basis of authority while claiming "to be different from his predecessor in that he thinks scientifically and despises dogma."[62]

Kerkut lists seven basic assumptions upon which the theory of evolution rests. These assumptions define the major lines of the Darwinian scheme of things yet all, according to Kerkut, are open to question. It is helpful that he states these premises as *assumptions,* for the average person struggling with these issues, listening to

---

61 G.A. Kerkut, *Implications of Evolution* (New York, Pergamon Press, 1960), vii.

62 Ibid., 3.

evolutionary claims, is likely to take them as "facts" developed from discovery. The seven assumptions are:

1. Non-living things gave rise to living material. Spontaneous generation occurred.
2. Spontaneous generation occurred only once.
3. Viruses, bacteria, plants and animals are all interrelated.
4. Protozoa gave rise to the Metazoa
5. The various invertebrate phyla are interrelated.
6. Within the vertebrates, fish gave rise to the amphibia, the amphibia to the reptiles, and the reptiles to the birds and mammals.

According to Kerkut, supporters of the theory of evolution generally hold these assumptions to be valid. However, he affirms that these assumptions, by their very nature, are *not capable of experimental verification* and at best depend upon limited circumstantial evidence.[63] It is interesting to read Kerkut's examination of the evidence for these assumptions. His discussion is characterized by a concern for the over-confident manner in which the General Theory of Evolution is presented in textbooks and science courses. His assessment of the evidence is punctuated with such words and phrases as "just an assumption," "belief rather than proof," "no definite evidence," "nothing definite is known," "tenuous and circumstantial," "insufficient," "not the type of evidence that would allow one to form a verdict of definite relationships." In one instance he refers to "science fiction" and goes on to say that "much of the evolution of the major groups of animals has to be taken on trust."[64] (Might we say *faith?*)

It is significant to recall that Kerkut wrote this book in the same era in which people like G.G. Simpson and Julian Huxley were promoting the worldview of evolutionism as a *necessary* perspective for a modern thinking person, while grounding their claims on the factual character of evolution. What is one to conclude, though,

---

63   Ibid., 7.
64   Ibid., 150-157

from Kerkut's presentation, other than that much of evolutionary thought is grounded in speculative presuppositions concerning the primordial past?

It is incumbent upon the scientific materialist, having denied the role of a creator in the world of nature, to offer a plausible case for the origin and development of life in purely physical terms or "naturalistic" elements. Kerkut's book demonstrated, I believe, that materialism had accomplished no such thing and that the claim that science has demolished biblical theism was, and continues to be, hollow dogmatism and a faith position in its own right.

The theist holds that God created the realm of nature. This is not a scientific statement, but that in itself does not deny its truth or its credibility. Nor does it deny the various chemical and biological processes actually observed to operate in nature, or the operations of natural law. It simply states the ultimate reason for the existence of life. The assumption of a creator does not, as is often alleged, demand that science bow to "supernaturalism." Even the concept of miracle—as presented in the Bible—does not deny the regularity of nature, causal sequences, or the possibility of natural knowledge. It is a beginning point. When one thinks about it, it becomes apparent that in order for anything to exist at all, *something must be eternal.* That eternal "something" is either intelligent or it is not. Materialists have in the past assumed the eternality of matter and energy—an eternally existing universe—but this beginning point is no less a matter of faith than the creation assumption of the theist. It is also much more difficult to hold in the wake of evidence from astronomy and physics that the universe did, indeed, have a beginning.

In the biblical view of things, nature is a clue to the presence of a creator. The heavens declare or reveal the glory of God, and the eternal power and divine nature of God is seen and understood through what has been made (Romans 1:20). The implications of this for scientific enterprise are friendly. If nature declares the power and glory of its creator, then why not study it? The theology is inviting. Yet, evolutionary scientists of the materialist camp insist that science, in order to proceed, must be tied to a naturalistic philosophy that denies the existence and creative action of God. Nevertheless, there is no evading the great issue of existence expressed in the human question as to why there is something rather than nothing. The materialist proposes that life, in some manner or other, came into being "on its own" without the initiative and guidance of intelligence, achieving along the way not only marvelous diversity of forms but reflective intelligence, consciousness, and a creature defined by a need to find "meaning." Many people find this picture of things to be incoherent with the known and observed nature of humanity.

According to evolutionary theory life arose with an initial simple organism or organisms, gradually evolving into more complex forms through millions of years. An almost incomprehensible amount of time is postulated for this to have happened. The fossil record is believed to present sufficient evidence[65] to support the theory of an ongoing trend toward complexity in life forms, with man being the "highest" product of the process. The process is seen to be the result of genetic mutations directed by natural selection, with life somehow arising out of non-living matter. Natural selection is the vital and animating concept of evolution—its necessary agent. Yet, this concept has itself been viewed more critically over the past few decades, with questions arising as to what it actually explains, if anything at all.

Critiques of natural selection

News of an emerging debate concerning the efficacy of natural selection as a meaningful concept was reported in *Harpers* magazine, February, 1976, in an article by Tom Bethell entitled "Darwin's Mistake." Bethell, who had majored in philosophy at Oxford and was at that time an editor for *Washington Monthly,* had more or

---

65 This is a matter of controversy, and a layperson looking into the issues will find contradictory assessments of the wealth of the fossil record. A very confident assessment is given by Kenneth R. Miller, *Finding Darwin's God* (New York: Harper Perennial Books, 2002). This book expresses a critique of scientific materialism as well as "intelligent design" by an author who is an enthusiastic theist (Roman Catholic) and Darwinian. A contrasting view of the fossil record is stated by Michael Denton, *Evolution: A Theory in Crisis* (Bethesda, Maryland: Adler and Adler, 1986).

less accepted the popular authority of evolution's triumph. Upon encountering the thought of Karl Popper, the famous philosopher of science, Bethell was awakened to the possibility that this acceptance was perhaps a bit too hasty. His article clarifies a major problem with the intellectual status of the concept of natural selection. The concept, it seems, doesn't really tell us anything. Natural selection defines a process whereby some types of creatures survive and others fail to do so. How do we know that it has been working? Well, by observing the creatures that survive.

This is known in philosophic language as a tautology, or a needless repetition of an idea, statement, or word in such a way that no useful information is conveyed. As the renowned geneticist T.H. Morgan (a Nobel Prize winner in Genetics) stated it: "For, it may appear little more than a truism to state that the individuals that are the best adapted to survive have a better chance of surviving than those not so well adapted to survive."[66]

Bethell expressed concern that, although this flaw in the concept of natural selection had been a very active debate in academic circles during the 1960s, very little word of it had leaked out. "What was it," Bethell asks, "that Darwin discovered?" Surprisingly, nothing of the same character as, say, Kepler's laws of planetary motion. Darwin's idea "was not a demonstration, but an argument . . . and natural selection was an idea, not a discovery."[67] His report goes on to present the ironies of noted evolutionists (Theodosius Dobzhansky, Gavin de Beer, G.G. Simpson, Julian Huxley) describing natural selection in terms of artistic activity, comparing its action to that of "a poet, a composer, a sculptor, Shakespeare—to the very notion of creativity that the idea of natural selection had originally replaced." That this is still done in popular presentations of evolution is demonstrated in various television specials on PBS and other nature-oriented programs that frequently speak of the "wisdom" of natural selection and evolutionary processes.

---

66 Quoted by Tom Bethell, "Darwin's Mistake," *Harpers*, (February, 1976). 72.

67 Ibid.

Bethell's *Harper's* article was followed in the popular press by other interesting inquiries that chipped away at the Darwinian edifice. *Life* magazine (April, 1982) published an excerpt from Francis Hitching's *The Neck of the Giraff: Where Darwin Went Wrong*.[68] Hitching distinguishes between *evolution* and *Darwinism*. "Darwinism is a theory that seeks to explain evolution. It has not, contrary to general belief, and despite very great efforts, been proved." In the article, Hitching challenges Darwinian "gradualism," and admits that the emerging picture of earth's history is accepting much more catastrophism than is allowed in orthodox uniformitarianism. (This reality has since been communicated to popular audiences via numerous television specials on ancient, and possibly future catastrophes of earth shattering proportions.)

The author makes the interesting point that the most forceful critique of Darwinian evolution is coming *not* from "creationists" but from the realm of mainstream science. Hitching concludes that Darwinian notions of natural selection have "been tested and found wanting" and that the concept can, at best, account for relatively minor variations within species. His concluding statement is somewhat startling: "The new biology is looking afresh at living things. . . . If, after more than a century, natural selection has been tested and found wanting, and if we are left with a sense of ignorance about origins, Darwin would not have minded." All this, at the very time when science textbooks were signaling to students that all research since Darwin confirmed Darwin's expectations!

Hitchings' perspective is echoed in an article by John Silber, President Emeritus of Boston University. Writing in *The New Criterion,* in the context of a critique of the tendency of science to become *scientism,* he reflects:

> The critical question for evolutionists is not about the *survival* of the fittest but about their *arrival.* Biologists arguing for evolution have been challenged by critics for more than a hundred years for their

---

68 See Francis Hitching, "Was Darwin Wrong?" in *Life* magazine, Vol. 5, No. 4 (April, 1982), 48-52.

failure to offer any scientific explanation for the arrival of the fittest."[69]

Native American scholar Vine Deloria, in a book in which he targets both evolutionists and creationists, calls attention to a lack of predictive power in natural selection. "One of the tenets of the scientific method is that concepts, doctrines, and dogmas should have some kind of predictive power. Many thinkers agree on a basic criticism of evolution: it is always applied *after the fact* to work data into a predetermined storyline." He quotes the Darwinian critic Richard Milton: "As a theory, natural selection makes no unique predictions but instead is used retrospectively to explain every outcome; and a theory that explains everything in this way explains nothing."[70]

Another curiosity-arousing article appeared in the Sunday edition of the *Chicago Tribune,* (January 6, 1985), entitled "Why Is Sex?" The article reports on a symposium concerning the origin and evolution of sex. The overall perspective outlined in this article is that Darwin's estimate that "the whole subject of sex is as yet hidden in darkness" still pertains today. Indeed, one biologist and author is quoted as saying that "the prevalence of sexual reproduction in higher plant and animals is inconsistent with current evolutionary theory."[71]

So what is the point here? I can discern someone pointing out that just because something is not presently understood, this in itself does not invalidate a research program or the larger Darwinian paradigm. I agree fully. The point, though, is that at the very time laypeople and students were being met with accusations of intellectual dishonesty or worse owing to skepticism about Darwinism's status as "fact," major problems had emerged in the edifice. Even fundamental aspects of

---

69 John Silber, "Science versus scientism," *The New Criterion,* November 2005, 12.

70 Vine Deloria, *Evolution, Creationism, and Other Modern Myths* (Golden, Co.: Fulcrum, 2002), 69.

71 Gardiner Morse, "Why Is Sex?" in *Chicago Tribune* (Section 4, Sunday January 6, 1985) 1.

reality were far from being clarified. This trend has continued and gained strength over succeeding decades.

Bethell and other subsequent authors (e.g. Michael Denton) attributed the ready acceptance of natural selection and its elevation to the status of scientific dogma to factors other than the persuasions of scientific evidence. The Victorian world in which Darwin lived was ready for an idea that seemed to bear out scientifically a vision of inevitable progress through the survival of the fittest. Nevertheless, it is amazing to find out that *no actual demonstration of natural selection* was forthcoming until almost 100 years after the publication of Darwin's *Origin of Species.* If nothing else, this demonstrates that the principle of natural selection—invoked for support of the atheist claims of Darwinian prophets—was accepted for its intrinsic attractiveness to certain worldview assumptions rather than because of objective scientific evidence.

This story is effectively summarized by Michael Denton , whose books *Evolution: A Theory in Crisis* (1985) and *Nature's Destiny* (1998) vividly reveal why an increasing number of scientists are braving ostracism and professional antagonism while challenging the familiar Darwinian orthodoxies. Denton relates the well-known story of how the operations of natural selection were first demonstrated in 1950 by British zoologist Bernard Kettlewell's study of peppered moths. This research is steadily invoked as a powerful support of the entire Darwinian edifice of belief. Natural selection does indeed operate in nature in the adaptations of organisms to environmental challenges. Nevertheless, this process is relatively trivial and falls far short of the kind of transformational, macroevolutionary change envisioned by the larger Darwinism. In Kettlewell's study, the moths changed color in response to environmental change, yet remained moths! To assert large, macroevolution from microevolution is an extrapolation that is speculative and problematic, for "it does not necessarily follow that, because a certain degree of evolution has been shown to occur, therefore any degree of evolution is possible."[72] Extrapolation from microevolution to macroevolution might prove to be as fallacious

---

72　Michael Denton, *Evolution: A Theory in Crisis* (Bethesda, Md.: Adler and Adler, 1986), 87.

as universalizing Newtonian physics was (Newton's laws describe the actions of nature in the realm of everyday, normally observed experience; they are inadequate, though, in the quantum world of physics).

Doubt concerning the validity of the microevolution-macroevolution extrapolation arises from what is actually observed in microevolution itself. In Darwinism, evolution takes place as natural selection acts upon accidental, chance genetic changes. Mutation is the "raw material" for the evolutionary process. As Julian Huxley explains, "natural selection converts accident into apparent design, randomness into organized pattern."[73] Yet according to Theodosius Dobzhansky, the vast majority of mutations that are actually observed are either harmful or useless to an organism, and "mutants that would make a major improvement of the normal organization in the normal environment are unknown."[74]

Dobzhansky admits that the deleterious effects of most mutations seem to present a problem for modern theories of evolution. The difficulty is alleviated somewhat, however, by the realization that useful mutations do, in fact, take place when organisms are placed in environments other than those in which they are normally found. Nevertheless, useful mutations are not observed in situations where species remain in their normal environment. The kind of transformational changes asserted by macroevolution *have never been observed*. The major classes of animal life change over time within their class, but what scientists actually observe in nature is that reptiles give birth only to reptiles, not to birds, and apes do not become humans. As Denton points out, the major types or classes of organisms are characterized by certain fundamental features that are uniquely theirs, and there is no credible evidence that these barriers have *ever been crossed*. In a discussion of nineteenth-century scientists who opposed Darwinian gradualism on the basis of typology (the perception that variation in organisms is conservative and limited to intratype change), Denton notes:

---

73 Huxley, *Evolution in Action,* 35
74 Dobzhansky, *Evolution, Genetics, and Man,* 135

All in all, the empirical pattern of existing nature conforms remarkably well to the typological model. The basic typological axioms—that classes are absolutely distinct, that classes possess unique diagnostic characters and that these diagnostic characteristics are present in fundamentally invariant form in all the members of a class—apply almost universally throughout the entire realm of life.[75]

Darwin, of course, predicted that sufficient transitional forms of life (popularly referred to as "missing links") would verify his theory of gradualistic transformation over time—hence the importance of the fossil record. Inasmuch as no such transitions have been directly observed, the hope lies in the past through the paleontological record. Here is where the average person looking into the issues is likely to be confused by diametrically opposed assessments of the fossil record by experts. Be this as it may, the simple reality is that the fossil record has been, from Darwin's day to ours, a matter of *scientific* controversy, with a number of outstanding scientists admitting that the transitional forms necessary for assuring the factual basis of Darwinian evolution are just not there. That this is the case is borne out by Stephen J. Gould's "punctuated equilibrium" theory, in which it is proposed that evolution occurs in "leaps," or "saltation," thereby conforming the evolutionary process to what the fossil record actually presents.

Very recently, too, we have seen the researcher of the much-noted new fossil "Ida," Dr. Jørn Hurum, declaring in a BBC television special that we now have "what we did not have before—a real missing link." Whether Ida proves anything about macroevolution remains to be seen. Despite much media hype in 2009 concerning the fossil discovery (made previously in 1983), professionals have been cautionary concerning the overblown claims made for its significance. Elwyn Simons of Duke University, a prominent paleoanthropologist, stated: "It's an extraordinarily complete, wonderful specimen, but

---

75   Denton, *Evolution: A Theory in Crisis,* 117.

it's not telling us too much that we didn't know before."[76] The stir surrounding Ida does, however, demonstrate the power of mass media to create impressions in people who read headlines. The truth is that the problematic nature of the fossil record, long recognized through the many years since Darwin, remains.

It is intriguing to know that at the mid-twentieth century, when the "fact" of macroevolution was being trumpeted by Darwinians like Julian Huxley, such an important evidence for the truth of Darwinian theory was lacking. This was frankly admitted by a leading origin-of-life researcher A. I. Oparin, who attributed the lack of transitional forms to the action of natural selection itself. "Natural selection has long ago destroyed and completely wiped off the face of the Earth all the intermediate forms of organization of primary colloidal systems and of the simplest living things."[77] This statement comes very close to saying—if not making it explicit— that natural selection has destroyed the evidence of its own working! This same appeal was injected into a conversation I had with a geologist colleague about these matters. But why, then, should the average person be exhorted to conform all his/her thinking to an evolutionary concept of life, as evolutionists propose? By definition, a belief in something for which there is no evidence is a superstition, and a belief in something that has destroyed the primary evidence of its reality is absurd. When one thinks about it, and recalls the tautological nature of the concept of natural selection, one suspects that there is something very odd about it.

Still, science students and teachers alike continue to speak easily about natural selection in macroevolutionary terms as if we were dealing with a self-evident truth. R.A. Fisher's assertion that natural selection was a "mechanism for generating an exceedingly high degree of improbability"[78] remains a trusted axiom. Time, here, has always been the hero of the plot in the evolutionist

---

76 William Moore, "The Primate Fossil 'Ida': The Science and the Hype," (http://www.wsws.org/articles/2009/jun2009/ida-j13.shtml) June 13, 2009.

77 A.I. Oparin, *Origin of Life* (New York, Dover Publications, 1953), 251.

78 cited by Julian Huxley, *Evolution in Action*, 40.

narrative and is seen as giving natural selection the opportunity to generate admittedly improbable results. As Huxley states: "A little calculation demonstrates how incredibly improbable the results of natural selection can be when enough time is available."[79] This claim, however, is not without its own problems, as becomes clear in the wake of mathematical and probabilistic studies of evolution that have arisen over the past 40 years.

Some interesting numbers

The big question has always been how a completely natural process of random, chance activity serving no goal or end moves on from the simplest protein (or even gets there in the first place) to creatures like bears, horses, apes, and ultimately human beings, and then such extraordinary creatures as people like Michelangelo, Bach, Einstein, etc., not to mention even the most ordinary person's mental and spiritual being. Huxley himself wrote of the "fantastic odds" involved in the evolution of such entities, stating a figure of one thousand multiplied to the millionth power! "One with three million noughts after it is the measure of the unlikeliness of a horse—the odds against it happening at all. No one would bet on anything so improbable happening; and yet it *has* happened. It has happened, thanks to the workings of natural selection and the properties of living substance which make natural selection inevitable."[80] Of course natural selection is supposed to overcome such improbability, but if natural selection really explains so little and is held to be a meaningless tautology, what are we left with except randomness and chance as the raw essence of evolution—Jacques Monod's cosmic "Monte Carlo game?"

Here, the role of probability studies as applied to evolution arises as a significant factor. These studies emerged as serious inquiries in the 1960s with the development of computer technology. These studies raised serious issues in regard to what had always been regarded as a comfortable time-span accepted as adequate for overcoming the improbabilities inherent in macroevolution. The idea stated the

79 Ibid., 41

80 Ibid., 41-42.

premise that given enough time, anything could happen. Princeton biologist Harold F. Blum, writing before the probability studies had come on the scene, refers to the extent of time available for the emergence of life as "inconceivable" and "lavish," and states that this consideration is vital to a proper perspective on the origin of life.[81] More recently, Michael Ruse notes that the time-span of billions of years of earth's history is more than enough for the "leisurely" progress of evolution to have occurred.[82]

Is there really enough time, even in 4.5 billion years, for an undirected, random, mindless evolutionary process to drive itself from the beginnings to where we are today?

It has been over fifty years since this question began to be asked. It directed the important studies carried out at the Wistar Institute of Anatomy and Biology, University of Pennsylvania in 1966. At this symposium, "the computational power of computers . . . revealed how improbable it was for a random mix of particles to produce a functionally designed organism."[83] The purpose of the conference, which was attended by some of the world's most accomplished and prominent mathematicians and biologists, was to study the question of the mathematical probability of evolutionary theory. The mathematicians were not impressed at the possibilities. Dr. Marcel Schutzenberger of the University of Paris declared "we believe it is not conceivable." Murray Eden, one of the leading Americans (MIT) attending stated that the randomness posited in the Neo-Darwinian system was highly implausible and that "an adequate theory of evolution must await the discovery and elucidation of new natural laws—physical, physio-chemical and biological."[84]

Commenting upon Dr. Eden's remarks, the *Philadelphia Inquirer* of April 26, 1966, stated that "his argument, in effect, was that the

---

81 Harold F. Blum, *Time's Arrow and Evolution* (New Jersey, Princeton University Press, 3rd edition, 1968; orig. pub. 1951), 51-52.

82 Michael Ruse, *The Creation-Evolution Controversy* (Cambridge, Harvard University Press, 2005), 87

83 Larry Witham, *By Design*, 23.

84 *Mathematical Challenges to the Neo-Darwinian Interpretation of Evolution* (Philadelphia: Wistar Institute Press,1967). The statements quoted here are cited by Jeremy Rifkin, *Algeny* (New York: The Viking Press, 1983), 154-155.

guts of evolutionary theory—Charles Darwin's concept of 'natural selection,' also known as survival of the fittest—breaks down in light of recent basis of inheritance." Relative to the formation of hemoglobins, "Dr. Eden used calculations to suggest that the whole period of life on earth—three billion years—would have to be extended millions of times for this single evolution to occur by simple 'natural selection' of random accidental changes."[85]

It is anyone's guess as to whether the average student in a college science course today is even aware of this study and its implications, although my guess is that they are not informed about it. Still, the numbers that come out of this study and subsequent investigations are staggering. We find, in fact, that one can concede the vast time scale assigned to earth's history and still not "have enough time," a realization that renders irrelevant the quirky attempts of some special creationists to establish an earth that is only 10,000 or so years old. According to James. F. Coppedge, Director of Probability Research in Biology (Northridge, California) the required time is just not there. Coppedge, in his interesting book *Evolution: Possible or Impossible,* [86] calculates the odds for the chance formation of the simplest protein as 1 in 10^{54}.

This is a chance factor of a million trillion trillion trillion trillion to one that not a single protein molecule of all that ever existed on earth would by chance be in the correct order for an insulin molecule. Assuming a five-billion year old earth, with amino acid chains forming at a fantastically rapid rate even beyond what known evidence would justify, the odds against the chance formation of an average protein molecule is 10 to 1^{161}, a number with 161 zeroes. This figure is the conclusion after making fourteen very generous concessions to help the materialist position. The odds against one minimum *set* of proteins happening in the entire history of the earth are calculated as 10^{119775} to 1. And even then, we would not have arrived at life. Furthermore, the probability for a minimum set of

---

85 Cited by James Reid, in *God, the Atom, and the Universe* (Grand Rapids: Zondervan Publishing House, 1968), 198.

86 James F. Coppedge, *Evolution: Possible or Impossible* (Grand Rapids: Zondervan Publishing House, 1973), 102-103.

the required 239 protein molecules for the smallest theoretical life is 1 in 10^{119879}. This would require many times over the assumed age of the earth. Coppedge's analyses are those of a believer in special creation; however, they are similar in their astonishing numbers to those of the evolutionist prophet Julian Huxley. Indeed, we may readily understand why Richard Dawkins famously employs the image of "Mount Improbable" in his discussions of evolution.

These numbers are far beyond the realm of possibility as defined by the world of statistics. Not surprisingly, probability studies have come under energetic criticism. Generally, the counter-argument is that "mere chance" is not a valid assumption, that natural selection overcomes the element of chance. Nevertheless, the mathematical researchers were simply taking up the claim set forth by evolutionary materialists themselves (e.g. Bertrand Russell, Jacques Monod) that the systems of nature are "accidental" and that humanity has emerged in the universe *"only by chance"* (Monod).

Richard Carrier takes up the issues in a critique of Coppedge, Eden, and the Wistar Institute[87] in a discussion in which he assumes what looks like a kind of "simple organism of the gaps" argument, claiming that just because we don't know of any simple organisms at present does not mean that we might not learn of one in the future. Still, mathematical arguments persist, and they have become more interesting over more recent years in the wake of new discoveries in the realm of molecular biology, which has revealed that there really isn't any such thing as a "simple" organism. Even the individual cell, the combinations of which make up living things, cannot be said to be "simple." Michael Denton gives us a vivid picture of the individual cell and how we would describe it if we were to use the language of technology:

> We would see that nearly every feature of our own advanced machines had its analogue in the cell: artificial languages and their decoding systems, memory banks for information storage and retrieval,

87 See Richard Carrier, "Are The Odds Against the Origin of Life Too Great To Accept?" (http://www.infidels.org/library/modern/richard_carrier/addenaB/html)

elegant control systems regulating the automated assembly of parts and components, error fail-safe and proof-reading devices utilized for quality control, assembly processes involving the principle of prefabrication and modular construction. In fact, so deep would be the feeling of *déjà-vu,* so persuasive the analogy, that much of the terminology we would use to describe this fascinating molecular reality would be borrowed from the world of late twentieth-century technology.[88]

Historical skepticism: a lost story?

Denton's ground-breaking book, *Evolution: A Theory in Crisis,* is important for the student not only for its evidential arguments calling into question the standard Darwinian doctrines, but for clarifying a point of which many laypeople are unaware—that *there has always been a scientific case against Darwinian concepts of evolution.* It is invariably assumed that the only opposition to Darwinian claims came from the realm of religion, that the "religionists" were the dogmatists, afraid of new knowledge, standing in the path of true learning, etc. Richard Dawkins and others of the "new atheists" are keen in their repetition of this mythology.

Denton notes that during Darwin's own time the most vigorous opposition to Darwin came from other scientists who did not see adequate evidence, and that "throughout the past century there has always existed a significant minority of first-rate biologists who have never been able to bring themselves to accept the validity of Darwinian claims."[89] Among those cited by Denton are people who attended a 1969 conference—the Alpbach Symposium. At this conference were world renowned authorities in various scientific fields, including Swedish neurobiologist Holgar Hyden, zoologists Paul Weiss and W.H. Thorpe, and child psychologist Jean Piaget. Arthur Koestler, the conference organizer, had invited them specifically because they

---

88 Michael Denton, *Evolution: A Theory in Crisis,* 329
89 Ibid., 327.

shared the discontent with Darwinian orthodoxies. Students reading textbooks, however, are not made aware of this historic and persistent questioning, and "dialogues" are almost invariably cast in the form of a "religion vs. science" confrontation.

Is it possible that the mainstream of academic science has indeed been involved in a process of active suppression of views questioning the triumphant dogma of Darwinian orthodoxy? Just such an assessment is offered by W.R. Thompson, Director of the Commonwealth Institute of Biological Control, Ottawa, in an introduction to the Everyman's Library edition of *Origin of Species* (1967). Thompson, who was an eminent Canadian entymologist, calls attention to the great divergence of opinion among scientists concerning not only the causes of evolution but the actual process itself. "This divergence exists because *the evidence is unsatisfactory* [emphasis mine]."

> It is therefore right and proper to draw the attention of the non-scientific public to the disagreements about evolution. But some recent remarks of evolutionists show that they think this unreasonable. This situation, where scientific men rally to the defense of a doctrine they are unable to define scientifically, much less demonstrate with scientific rigour, attempting to maintain its credit with the public by the suppression of criticism and the elimination of difficulties, is abnormal and undesirable in science.[90]

Stanley L. Jaki, a physicist and historian of science, concurs. In response to the claims of Sir Julian Huxley that Darwinism was fully accepted by the great majority of students of evolution, Jaki suggests that the lack of awareness of scientific skepticism concerning Darwinism is intentional, and substantially the result of craven and arbitrary claims to the effect that no "serious" scientist questions it. Jaki notes:

---

90   W.R. Thompson, Introduction to Charles Darwin's *Origin of Species* (London: J.M. Dent and Sons, EVERYMAN'S LIBRARY edition, 1967), xxii.

[P]hrases like 'great majority' are sufficiently vague to create the illusion that the minority is negligible qualitatively as well. This is far from being the case. Indeed, the persistence over four generations of a minority quantitatively not small and qualitatively most respectable, is quite a unique phenomenon in the history of modern science, in which the opposition to the main trend usually dies out with the generation of the original dissenters.[91]

Evidence of the active suppression of scientific critiques of evolution emerged at no less an institution than Oxford, in 1986, in which Darwinians engaged creationists in a program titled "A Critical Historical Perspective on the Argument About Evolution and Creation." The program was sponsored by the Oxford Union Debating Society and was presented in honor of the famous nineteenth-century Darwinist propagandist T.H. Huxley. Prominently featured on this occasion were the Oxford biologist Richard Dawkins and the creationist movement's most intellectually formidable spokesman A.E. Wilder-Smith. When the debate—which involved an audience vote as to the winner—aroused substantial support for the creationist side, the normal prominent reports to the press of the Oxford debates were suspended. Not only did 37% of the Oxford audience vote in favor of the creationist case, but Richard Dawkins broke the accepted protocols of the program by exhorting the audience to vote against the creationist position while making *ad hominem,* religion-based comments toward Dr. Wilder-Smith. All records of the debate were expunged from the Oxford Debating Society's records. It would appear that Wilder-Smith held his own quite well against Dawkins and that the substantial support shown for Wilder-Smith proved embarrassing. In his memoir *Journey Fulfilled* Wilder-Smith reflected:

In the end the creationists won some 114 of the votes from the voting public of about 300—which was quite surprising, as the Oxford Union represented

91   Stanley L. Jaki, *The Road of Science and the Ways To God,* 287-288.

the materialistic naturalistic evolutionary viewpoint of biogenesis. The debate was never published. . . . In December 1986, I received an inquiry from the Radcliffe Science Library, Oxford, asking if I had ever really held a Huxley Memorial Lecture on February 14, 1986. No records of my having held the lecture as part of the Oxford Union Debate could be found in any library. No part of the official media breathed a word about it. So total is the current censorship on any effective criticism of Neo-Darwinian science and on any genuine alternative.[92]

Origin of life issues

The response of the Darwinian establishment to the various lines of critique have varied, from ignoring the problem altogether and challenging the premises of the mathematical inquiries to making *ad hominem* attacks on dissenters. One especially intriguing response, however, has been to simply assert the "inevitability" of all that has happened on planet earth through evolution, thereby skirting the objections associated with "chance" effects. A.I. Oparin was one of the early advocates of this vision. In *The Chemical Origin of Life* (1964) he wrote that the origin of life on our Earth was not due to some "lucky chance" as had hitherto been believed, but that "it must be regarded as a natural and inevitable part of the general development of our planet.[93]

Oparin outlines the implications of the study of life's origin, and rightly affirms that the solutions posited for this problem have *consequences for our whole outlook on the world and human society.* Oparin recognizes that for many, the idea of divine creation has received a "mortal blow," having been ousted by science. Man is now forced to accommodate his thinking to the present achievements of

---

92 See "Fraudulent report at AAAS and the 1986 Oxford University Debate," (http://samizat.qc.ca/origines/debate_gc.htm)

93 A.I. Oparin, *The Chemical Origin of Life* (Springfield, Ill.: Charles C. Thomas Publisher, 1964), xi.

science, eschewing any "cosmological theories of the past."[94] Science is the single overriding principle with which humanity must now seek answers to our place in the universe.

Many modern scientists and laypeople accept this premise. For a Christian layperson like myself, the issue is *not* whether there is a chemical reality to the origin and nature of living systems—obviously there is. Again, the discovery of natural processes or "laws" pertaining to the natural world says nothing, one way or another, concerning the existence or non-existence of God. Yet, this seems to be the premise underlying the close connection that is drawn between evolutionary natural science and a purely naturalistic philosophy and materialistic worldview. But this is an assumed necessity, nothing more. Richard Dawkins claims that the realm of science leads an intelligent person inevitably and *necessarily* to the dismissal of theological belief as a "delusion." However, the discerning individual will see, here, mere opinion disguising itself in the wrappings of prestige associated with science.

Great media attention is given to origin-of-life research, and people in this field of study assert that the day is certain to come when life will be successfully synthesized in the laboratory. Underlying these efforts and stated hope is the belief that under certain conditions which are thought to have existed in the primitive earth, life was generated through "inevitable" chemical processes.

A moment's reflection may reveal, though, that an appeal to the "inevitability" of the process does not explain very much at all, and it may constitute little more than question-begging resting upon gratuitous assumptions. The doctrine of inevitability accomplishes nothing crucial for the question of the origin of life. The issues have to do with the origin of the properties of chemical substances themselves and the laws that they obey. Such properties and potentials are part of the entire design fabric of nature, and the questions that we have already confronted are simply pushed back one step further.

Dean Kenyon, an origin-of-life researcher originally inspired by Oparin, came to the realization that positing the inevitability of chemical bonds overlooked a deeper issue—the information elements

---

94   Ibid., xiv-xv.

in the processes that were crucial but which could not have been derived from chemical substances themselves. Similarly Michael Polanyi understood living systems as being driven by communications systems that "defy reduction to physical and chemical law. . . . Polanyi argued that, as with other systems of communication, the lower-level laws of physics and chemistry cannot explain the higher levels of DNA. DNA base sequencing cannot be explained by lower-level chemical laws or properties any more than the information in a newspaper headline can be explained by reference to the chemical properties of ink."[95]

Let us envision an actual occasion in which scientists accomplish the laboratory creation of a real living and self-replicating organism. What would be demonstrated in such an event? Common sense would see a demonstration of a planning intelligence (the experimenter), working retrospectively from a prior knowledge of life's chemistry, figuring out a way to put it all together. It is difficult to see, though, how this would prove anything relative to a purely naturalistic origin and evolution of life. One does not have to be an expert or even a scientist to realize this, but I'll let Michael Behe (Lehigh biology professor who arouses great indignation among Darwinists) make the point:

> [I]t may . . . be possible to arrange a local set of conditions that would lead to life. . . . If it succeeded, some would claim that it revealed that life needed no miracle. But in fact it would show the beginning of life needed a directing intelligence. . . . [I]t may be possible for scientists to select approximate physical conditions in the laboratory, and deliberately cause batches of certain mutations to occur at the right times, and that would be a scientifically interesting project. But without the intimate involvement of a directing intelligence, they would not come about in nature. [96]

---

95 Stephen C. Meyer, *Signature in the Cell,* 237-240.
96 Michael Behe, *The Edge of Evolution* (New York: Free Press, 2007), 216-217.

Something from nothing?

Reflective people may well conclude, or at least hold with intellectual integrity, that the claims that present-day scientific knowledge has "dealt a mortal blow" to theistic belief are overblown. The materialist claims that life brought itself into being out of an eternally existing "something" that was not, in fact, living. We proceed, here, with some other aspects of this idea and its problematic nature. Two major considerations are in view, much discussed in the larger conversations regarding creation and evolution, which I'll pose as two questions.

1.) Does not the idea of evolution contradict the second law of thermodynamics, which states that matter, left to itself, has an inherent and natural tendency toward disorder?

2.) How could life have arisen from non-living substance, when life as it is actually observed can arise only from life itself?

The second law of thermodynamics is also known as the law of *entropy*. The laws of thermodynamics describe energy relationships. The first law states that energy, at the present time, is neither being created nor destroyed. The second law states that the amount of energy available to do useful work is getting smaller. The measure of unavailable energy is called entropy. Therefore, entropy represents a state of disorder and equilibrium, and *this state is the one of greater probability*. Ordered systems tend to descend into disorder and chaos. In everyday experience we may see this tendency operating. The human body inevitably declines in its ability to function and then dies. Machines of all types are in need of watchful care and maintenance to keep them from breaking down. Even so, they eventually need to be replaced.

Matter, then, left to its natural tendencies proceeds to a state of disorder, or entropy. All *ordered* systems represent, conversely, reductions in entropy. This reality arouses an important consideration. In human experience, all reductions in entropy are the direct result of intelligence acting upon matter. In view of this, evolution seems to teach a situation that directly contradicts a universally accepted natural law—the second law of thermodynamics. If the inherent tendency of matter is toward disorder, how could the world and its complex life system have arisen *on its own?*

Indeed, if we were to extrapolate from our own experience toward a theory of origins, the most natural procedure would be in the direction of creative intelligence, because it is more in accord with what we actually observe. The materialist must face up to the problem of entropy—something that creationists charge they have not been able or willing to do.

Nevertheless, disagreements arise as to the "problem" of the second law, even among Christian apologists, and certainly there is a broad perception among theists and materialists that evolution and entropy are not necessarily in irreconcilable contradiction. Still, there is recognition that it must be considered at some point along the way. This is because of the apparent "closed circle" involved in the problem of the origin of life itself.

Evolutionists defuse the argument from the second law of thermodynamics by pointing out that the earth is, in fact, an open system, whereas the law applies only to closed systems. As an open system, earth receives outside energy from the sun. Therefore, entropy could decrease in the earth at the expense of the total system of the universe. That is, total entropy is on the increase while decreasing in local situations. This interpretation is accepted by some Christian scientists, but is strongly opposed by others. Richard H. Bube, a well-known Christian writer, agrees that "life does not violate the second law of thermodynamics, for the production and maintenance of life on earth is costing the universe in entropy increases which exceed the entropy decrease associated with living systems."[97] But, whereas Bube does not see any conflict between evolution and entropy, Christian apologist Bernard Ramm states the view that they "are headed in opposite directions."

> Entropy is the gradual equalization of molecular velocities through random collisions, and it is degenerative in the sense that the physical state

---

97 Richard H. Bube, *The Human Quest* (Waco, Tex.: Word Books, 1971), 186.

of energy levels is increased. Life is possible only
if miraculously these two features of entropy are
reversed, and certainly entropy is the more basic and
universal law than evolution. [98]

Creationist writers stress the apparent contradiction between
evolutionary theory and the second law. The "open system" argument
leaves unanswered the question as to how solar energy could have
stimulated life initially without the presence of a synthesizing
mechanism. A.E. Wilder-Smith points to this problem as a crucial
missing factor in materialist theories of origins, for without a
previously existing metabolic "motor" that could utilize solar energy
in the first place, that energy would go nowhere.[99] Before the energy
of the sun can be brought in to overcome the seeming conflict
between entropy and evolution, the origins of the complex process of
synthesizing energy much be explained. Wilder-Smith, commenting
on the "boot-straps" materialist vision, argues that the big question is
not how cells read codes, but how cells got coded in the first place.

> The difficulty with [the randomness, selection, and
> long time spans explanation] is that scientists have
> never experimentally found a trace of this self-
> ordering-up-to-life property in isolated non-living
> matter. In fact the second law of thermodynamics
> expresses the universal scientific belief that it does
> not exist! . . . Wherever codes, order, reduction
> of entropy or even reading of codes (translating
> them into 'reality') are seen, there we know from
> absolutely uniform experience that intelligence has
> been at work somewhere down the line. [100]

---

98 Bernard Ramm, *The Christian View of Science and Scripture* (Grand Rapids:Eerdmans,1954), 193.

99 A.E. Wilder-Smith, *The Creation of Life: A Cybernetic Approach to Evolution*, 71.

100 Ibid., 222-224.

These reflections call attention to the fundamental issue. How could life have arisen from non-living substance, when life as it is actually observed arises only from a prior living system?

The basic mystery is clarified by Harold F. Blum:

> The riddle seems to be: How, when no life existed, did substances come into being which, today, are absolutely essential to living systems, yet which can only be formed by those systems?[101]

Blum wrote of this dilemma in 1951 even before the famous Miller-Urey experiment (1953), which was trumpeted sensationally in the media as the "creation of life" in a test tube. So the problem may seem out-of-date, given the great amount of research into the origin of life that has been carried out since then. More recent statements by origins researchers would indicate that the mystery is as stringent as ever. Andy Knoll, Professor of Biology at Harvard, stated in a PBS interview for a NOVA program (May 3, 2004) that in respect to the origin of life issue "I think we have to admit that we're looking through a glass darkly here," and that "we don't know how life started on this planet." Similarly, origins researcher Antonio Lazcano makes the same point as Blum made previously: "Life could not have evolved without a genetic mechanism—one able to store, replicate, and transmit to its progeny information that can change with time. . . . Precisely how the first genetic machinery evolved also persists as an unresolved issue. The exact pathway for life's origin may never be known."[102]

These statements recapitulate the assessment of French biologist and evolution prophet Jacques Monod, who treats this subject in *Chance and Necessity.* Writing of the processes leading up to the formation of the primitive cell that must have existed in the far past, Monod states:

---

101 Harold F. Blum, *Time's Arrow and Evolution* (New Jersey: Princeton University Press, 3rd edition; orig. pub. 1951), 65.

102 Lazcano's statements are from "The Origins of Life," in *Natural History* (February, 2006). Both Knoll and Lazcano are cited by Anthony Flew, *There is A God*, 130.

It is here that one reaches the real "sound wall," for we have no idea what the structure of a primitive cell might have been. The simplest living system known to us, the bacterial cell, a tiny piece of extremely complex and efficient machinery, attained its present state of perfection perhaps a billion years ago. Its overall chemical ground plan is the same as that of all other living beings. It employs the same genetic code and the same mechanisms of translation as do, for example, human cells.[103]

We note a vital concern here, and that is the degree of complexity present in living things, even on the simplest levels. The idea of an evolutionary process moving from "simple to complex" organisms is difficult to sustain in view of research since Darwin's time, although that perception is still prevalent among most laypeople and students. Monod observes, though, that there is nothing "primitive" about them at all, and that without the help of fossils it is impossible to reconstruct the supposed evolutionary processes in their development. The major problem, however, is the origin of the genetic code itself and its translation mechanism.

The code is meaningless unless translated. The modern cell's translating machinery consists of at least fifty macromolecular components which are themselves coded in DNA: the code cannot be translated otherwise than by products of translation. . . . When and how did this circle become closed? It is exceedingly difficult to imagine.[104]

Monod considered this riddle to be "Herculean." Blum thought that it might never be solved short of scientists making direct observations with the aid of a time machine![105] It is also intriguing to see how close their views on this are to the arguments set forth

103 Jacques Monod, *Chance and Necessity*, 142.
104 Ibid., 146
105 Blum, 171.

by the creationist A.E. Wilder-Smith. Currently, as of this writing, the mystery of life's origin increasingly considers the mystery of information. Life functions according to codes and information, and all human experience of such realities assumes the reality of intelligence as a creative source and support. Increasingly, information theory is at the core of origin-of-life discussions.

Life as we know it demands quite specific conditions. Claiming that it is "inevitable" given the right conditions explains nothing, and constitutes an invalid circular argument. From the initial premise that under the right conditions life will arise and develop from chemical processes comes the observation that life has arisen and developed. Therefore, the "conclusion" is drawn that life arose and developed from non-living substances because the conditions were right.

A universe made for us?

The deeper question, though, is *why* such conditions should be in place at all, and it is this type of question that fuels the greater human quest for meaning. In this regard, recent decades have seen the growth in exploration of what is called "the anthropic principle" and "the fine-tuned universe." There is general acceptance, even by evolutionists, that the phenomenon of life as we see it is improbable; yet, we are here. Even materialists sometimes will be found resorting to the concept of the "miraculous" in response to this hard fact.

The "anthropic principle" defines the observation that the entire universe seems to have been purposefully set up for carbon-based life and, more specifically, an observing consciousness capable of studying it. The principle recognizes that various physical "constants" in the realm of nature must be exactly as they are in order for any life at all to exist. If even one of them were varied in the slightest degree no life would be possible.

One of the fullest explications of these issues is presented in Michael Denton's *Nature's Destiny: How the Laws of Biology Reveal Purpose in the Universe* (1998), a follow up to his earlier work previously cited. Denton explains:

The physical and chemical properties of the fundamental constituents of the cell, such as water, carbon dioxide, the bicarbonate buffer, oxygen, DNA, proteins, the transitional metals, the cell membrane, etc., are systematically reviewed to show that the existence of carbon-and-water-based cellular life depends critically on a number of remarkable adaptations in the properties of many of life's basic constituents. What is particularly striking is that, in almost every case, each constituent appears to be the only available or unique candidate for its particular biological role and, further, gives every appearance of being ideally fit not in one or two but in all its physical and chemical characteristics.[106]

The essence of the anthropic principle is that the universe looks like a "put up job" specifically designed for intelligent human life. Denton notes that this understanding, in which human consciousness exists in a natural environment "fitted" for it, is actually more compatible with the older theological worldview than it is with the "mediocrity" worldview of modern science, which suggests that the earth and humanity are of little significance in the larger context of the universe. The emerging anthropic universe constitutes a significant challenge to traditional materialist ideas of chance and random selection, and was a major factor in the eventual acceptance of a divine mind by Anthony Flew, one of the twentieth century's most prominent atheist philosophers.

Flew arrived at a form of deism in his worldview largely as a result of his reflections on scientific evidences.[107] One materialist/evolutionist commented on the problem by noting that "without

---

106 Michael Denton, *Nature's Destiny: How The Laws of Biology Reveal Purpose in the Universe* (New York, The Free Press, 1998), xiv. Michael Denton is Senior Research Fellow in Human Molecular Genetics at the University of Otago in New Zealand.

107 See Anthony Flew, with Roy Abraham Varghese, *There Is A God: How The World's Most Notorious Atheist Changed His Mind* (New York, HarperCollins, 2007).

any explanation of nature's fine-tunings we will be hard pressed to answer the ID [intelligent design] critics. One might argue that the hope that a mathematically unique solution will emerge is as faith-based as ID."[108]

Interpretations of this apparent "fine-tuning" tend in the direction of theism (or at least some form of divine intelligence/designer) or an acceptable alternative within the context of pure naturalism. One of the more sensational notions is the positing of a "multiverse," a concept of countless universes all defined by their different laws and in which ours is one of countless possibilities. Therefore our systems of life are in fact *probable*, rather than improbable! The multiplicity of universes overcomes the probability difficulties inhering in mathematical applications to evolution, because (as the thinking goes) in a multiverse of countless universes *anything can happen and most certainly will,* and we just happen to be in the one that is appropriate for us. As the mathematician and philosopher David Berlinsky expresses it, the multiverse proposal "dissolves improbabilities," and "dilutes the acrid acid of improbability."[109]

If this idea seems a bit strained, or even crazy, consider that it is advocated by one of the allegedly three greatest intellectuals in the world today, biologist and atheist prophet Richard Dawkins. Dawkins insists that the anthropic principle is actually an *alternative* to a design concept (it is, in fact, applied in support of both theism and materialism). He grants that the origin of life is highly improbable, but that in a multiverse—or even in the vastness of our own universe—the "stroke of luck" needed will almost certainly occur and we are the result. He appeals, like Huxley and Richard Carrier, to natural selection as the inevitable (non-luck) agency driving or lifting life along the road up "Mount Improbable" in a "one-way street to improvement."[110]

---

108 Leonard Susskind, as quoted by David Berlinski in *The Devil's Delusion: Atheism and Its Scientific Pretensions* (New York, Crown Forum, 2008), 135.

109 David Berlinski, *The Devil's Delusion: Atheism and Its Scientific Pretensions*, 124

110 Richard Dawkins, *The God Delusion*, 162-173.

Dawkins's position is ironic, for although he insists that the "God hypothesis" is irrational and unworthy because there is no evidence for it, he appeals to a multiverse (and in fact finds it to be "beautiful") for which there is no evidence! It would seem that the whole approach throws the evolutionist finally back to luck, for, as Colorado State philosopher Ralston Holmes has observed, "to invent myriads of other worlds in order to explain how this one came to be seems to show an addiction to randomness in one's explanatory scheme."[111] Which brings us back to fundamental questions of "how" and "why?"

Even if it be granted that once life got its "lucky" start it is then guided inevitably by the law of natural selection (that "counter-intuitive thing" that has the "power to tame improbability"), we are left with the most basic question: where did *that* law come from, why should *it* be there, capable of being discerned and observed and interpreted by a thinking consciousness? And the more we consider the question it becomes apparent that we are entering into the realm of *faith,* whatever our worldview may be. As Anthony Flew expresses it, mindful of Dawkins' challenge that the origin of God needs an explanation:

> Dawkins and the others ask, "Who created God?" Now, clearly, theists and atheists can agree on one thing: if anything at all exists, there must be something preceding it that always existed. How did this eternally existing reality come to be? The answer is that it never came to be. It always existed. Take you pick: God or universe. Something always existed.[112]

For theist and atheist alike, dealing with the meaning of life begins with the contemplation of *something* that is *eternal,* something that is by definition beyond the realm of time and causality, a reality that is by its nature beyond the reach of scientific method.

---

111 Ralston Holmes III, "Shaken Atheism: A Look at the Fine-Tuned Universe," *Christian Century* (December 3, 1986), 1094.
112 Anthony Flew, *There Is A God,* 165

It bears noting, too, that the concept of a multiverse is in no way the exclusive province of atheism or something that should, in and of itself, be seen as eroding the basis of theistic belief. For Stephen Hawking, the multiverse concept supports his view that the apparent design of nature is simply a natural result of our being here in this particular universe; nevertheless, "we human beings . . . are mere collections of fundamental particles of nature" [113] who just happen to be here. Mathematical physicist Frank J. Tipler, however, sees it differently, positing the vision of a multiverse as necessitated by the known laws of physics while affirming that vision as expressing Christian Trinitarian theism.[114] Tipler notes that the affirmation of multiple worlds is consonant with the Nicene Creed, which mentions worlds "visible and invisible." Looked at this way, the multiverse idea is really not all that new. In any event, there seems to be little about the idea that would compel a person, out of intellectual necessity, toward a materialistic atheism.

Consciousness

All of this, of course, does not even get close to the issues of human consciousness, or even general consciousness throughout nature. Consciousness is a phenomenon that transcends physical realities. Flew comments:

> The phenomena in question range from code and symbol-processing systems and goal-seeking, intention-manifesting agents at one end to subjective awareness, conceptual thought, and the human self at the other. The only coherent way to describe these phenomena is to say that they are different dimensions of being that are supraphysical in one way or another. They are totally integrated with the physical and yet radically "new."[115]

---

113 Stephen Hawking, *The Grand Design* (New York, Bantam Books, 2010), 181

114 Frank J. Tipler, *The Physics of Christianity* (New York, Doubleday, 2007).

115 Anthony Flew, *There Is A God*, 182.

For Flew, the answer to the question of the origin of self-directing consciousness, characterized as it is by subjective awareness, a sense of self, etc., is that it can come only from something that in fact possesses these qualities. "If we are centers of consciousness and thought who are able to know and love and intend and execute, I cannot see how such centers could come to be from something that is itself incapable of all these activities."[116] Flew comes to this conclusion from simple experience and an actual appeal to what we observe in nature itself. Greater phenomena do *not* derive from lesser phenomena.

Materialists will counter this by pointing out that life, including mental life, is connected to physical and chemical processes. Anybody who takes an anti-depressant drug knows that consciousness, mental energy, directedness, volition, joy, etc. have a chemical base. So, does not this indicate an ultimately materialist explanation? Here we encounter what is generally recognized as the "reductionist fallacy."

Reductionism is the intellectual process whereby a complex phenomenon is "reduced" to one, single level of understanding. But this is simplistic, and assumes that because we may know something about one aspect of a phenomenon (i.e. the chemical basis of life) that we have the whole picture. It is a bit like studying the chemical properties of the pigment, vehicles, and support base of Leonardo da Vinci's *Mona Lisa* and assuming, on that basis alone, that one understood its true nature. This is the fallacy that Donald M. Mackay, a brain researcher, calls "nothing buttery."

> Nothing-buttery is characterized by the notion that by reducing any phenomenon to its components you not only explain it, but *explain it away*. You can debunk love, or bravery, or sin for that matter, by finding the psychological or physiological mechanisms underlying the behavior in question.[117]

---

116 Ibid., 183.
117 Donald M. Mackay, *The Clockwork Image* (Downers Grove, Ill.:, 1974), 43.

Atheist writer Sam Harris makes a similar point in a discussion of consciousness, in a statement that suggests, perhaps, why his book *The End of Faith* has proved a bit unsettling to his materialist readers. "It is true enough to say that, in physical terms, you are little more than an eddy in a great river of life," he writes. Then, this:

> "To examine the body of a person, its organs and tissues, cells and intestinal flora . . . is to be confronted by a world that bears no more evidence of an overriding conscious intelligence than does the world at large. Is there any reason to suspect, when observing the function of mitochondria within a cell, or the twitching of muscle fibers in the hand, that there is a mind, above and beyond such processes, thinking 'L'état c' est moi'?"[118]

This is a most interesting observation and question. Whereas Harris perhaps means to make a point of reducing the phenomenon of consciousness to ultimate materialism, his question can be interpreted otherwise as well. Clearly his words imply that the mere materials observed cannot really account for the reality—consciousness—that is the object of concern. A theist might inquire as to why this disjunction might not be applied to our understanding of the world at large and the larger phenomena of human life. Returning to my initial example of an audience listening to a symphony concert, can we really explain the mental and emotional responses by reducing the whole experience to the wood and strings of the instruments, or the secretions and gases active inside the physical bodies of the performers and listeners?

Indeed, thoughtful people may detect a grinding contradiction here. The larger worldview of evolutionism offers the premise that there is no ultimate purpose or meaning to life. In this sense, it affirms Macbeth's lament: "Life's but a walking shadow, a poor player that struts and frets his hour upon the stage and then is heard no more: it is a tale told by an idiot, full of sound and fury, signifying

---

118 Sam Harris, *The End of Faith*, 210-211.

nothing."[119] But people do not actually live that way, even the most convinced materialist. If one were to be fully convinced of this view of life, though, why would one pay any attention to investigating the mysteries of nature, or be committed to anything other than the exercise of power? Ironically, it is highly unlikely that science itself could ever have arisen on the basis of evolutionism's fundamental doctrines.

Summary

Let us, at this point, review what has been argued in the preceding pages.

The discussion began, in Part I, with a broad definition of the worldview of evolutionism, a philosophic view of life that claims scientific support from the evidences of microevolution and the extrapolation from microevolution into macroevolution, or the "larger Darwinism." This view of life *insists* that evolution points *necessarily* in the direction of atheism, and that any intelligent, modern person must in fact realize this. This outlook is supported in the historic traditions of Darwinian thinkers, from Ernst Haeckel and T.H. Huxley in the nineteenth century through twentieth-century thinkers like George Gaylord Simpson, Bertrand Russell, Julian Huxley, continuing more recently in the writings of "science-demands-atheism" thinkers in the mold of Richard Dawkins, William Provine, Sam Harris, and countless and nameless professors throughout academe. It is this thesis that begs examination. Does, in fact, theistic belief wither and die for educated and intelligent people in the face of the overwhelmingly convincing concepts animating the Darwinian view of life?

In Part II I have focused on the issue of evidence. Does the actual evidence of macroevolution lend sufficient support to the worldview of evolutionism in such a way that necessitates the allegiance of intelligent people? As we have seen, not only is there a vigorous *scientific* critique of standard Darwinian concepts of life's origin and

---

119 William Shakespeare, "Macbeth," in W.G. Clark and W. Aldis Wright, ed., *The Complete Works of William Shakespeare*, vol. 2 (Garden City, N.Y.: Doubleday), 813

development, this critique has *always existed* and has actually gained strength in recent decades. It is a fallacy to think that the only way to approach the issues is to pose a "science vs. religion" or a "faith vs. reason" template.

Clearly, there is much of interest in the current controversies over evolution. Despite the insistence that there is no basis for controversy, that any perception of legitimate controversy is nothing but the product of grinding ignorance (e.g. Richard Dawkins), these issues are real, and they animate the professional life and researches of many people quite qualified to raise questions. Students, at some point and in some context, deserve a reasonable exposure to these matters rather than to be met with the nervous, irritated denunciations that are more typical.

The reader will decide whether or not the doctrine of evolution is on firm enough grounds to compel the allegiances of intelligent people to a necessary atheism. For me, it is clear that 150 years after Darwin there is still an on-going, meaningful, and increasingly "hot" debate about the viability of the Darwinian picture, that this debate involves professional people in various scientific disciplines as well as philosophy, history, and the arts, and that the "overthrow" of theology on the basis of the assured truths of Darwinism is, to say the least, overblown. For a Christian, it is important to realize that whatever reasons may be stated for the embrace of atheism or the rejection of the Christian message and worldview, evolution is not a very good one. My own suspicion is that that rationale probably masks other reasons of a more emotional, personal nature, but it sounds better to offer one's position as resting on "science," "reason," "objective knowledge," and so forth.

Evolutionism provides a powerful narrative, as defined in Part I of this essay. That it lends meaning and its own consolations to its believers is not to be denied. As Edward O. Wilson has stated, we should "make no mistake about the power of scientific materialism. It presents the human mind with an alternative mythology that until now has always, point for point in zones of conflict, defeated traditional religion."[120] Nor is the mere fact that there are missing

---

120 quoted in Michael Ruse, *The Evolution-Creation Struggle,* 206.

elements in evolution terribly significant in itself, for there are problems, apparent inconsistencies, paradoxes, anomalies and voids in every philosophy or worldview, Christianity included. I think, however, that there is enough evidence from enough professional people to indicate that the problems within Darwinism are significant, and that teachers owe students and their own colleagues a reasonable opportunity to look into these matters in a spirit of free inquiry.

In the mid-twentieth century, at a time when the "fact" of evolution was being promoted full-bore as a support for an increasingly attractive and compelling secularism, the noted naturalist Loren Eisely wrote the following words:

> After having chided the theologian for his reliance on myth and miracle, science found itself in the unenviable position of having to create a mythology of its own: namely, the assumption that what, after long effort, could not be proved to take place today had, in truth, taken place in the primeval past.[121]

E.O. Wilson and Eisely are not alone in using the concept of "myth" in regard to evolution. J.D. Bernal wrote that where "so much is still speculative, it is difficult to give a coherent account that is at the same time soundly based in all points. . . . Yet . . . it must be told as a reasonable, continuous, hypothetical story, a myth of the origin of life."[122]

Statements like those above, and the perceptions of scientists of more recent presence clearly suggest that the designation of evolution as a *belief* is not far off the mark. We are not without good reason to suppose that we may in fact be making our way through an intellectual environment characterized by W.R. Thompson as a place

---

121 Loren Eisely, *The Immense Journey* (New York: Random House, 1957; orig. pub. 1946), 199

122 J.D. Bernal, *The Origin of Life* (Cleveland: World Publishing Co., 1967), 35.

of "fragile towers of hypotheses based on hypotheses, where fact and fiction intermingle in an inextricable confusion."[123]

The reader will recognize that the foregoing discussion makes no apologetic for the Christian faith. Whether there are good reasons to doubt or affirm the Christian gospel is a matter all its own, given *its* particular premises and evidences. That is another story often told by theologians, historians, biblical scholars, philosophers, and yes, even scientists. It begs pointing out, however, that the Christian belief system has been rigorously tested in the lives of its adherents and in the skeptical inquiries, even assaults, of its detractors, with special energies applied by skeptics over the past two centuries. These inquiries have focused on vital, not secondary matters, and theologians have responded to these energies with both foolish accusation and restrained wisdom and rational argument. Evolutionism, as modernity's major belief system and foundation of modern secularism's "post-Christian" world, must face up to and accept similar levels of inquiry.

---

123 W.R. Thompson, "Introduction" to EVERYMAN'S LIBRARY edition of *The Origin of Species,* xxiv.

Appendix I

Book Review
The Grand Design
by Stephen Hawking and Leonard Mlodinow (New York, Bantam, 2010)

Review by Richard Terrell

The current book of sensational discussion is Stephen Hawking's *The Grand Design*, written with fellow physicist Leonard Mlodinow. Hawking is the superstar of science in our time, and Mlodinow wrote scripts for "Star Trek." The book's release has fueled resurgent discussions about the question of God's existence, owing to the authors' claim that the existence of the universe, including the "why" questions formerly reserved for philosophy and theology, require no positing of a divine, creative intelligence.

The book is filled with fascinating descriptions of the strange and wonderful ways of nature. Although the discussion is "dumbed down" for the sake of generating a lay-audience for the book, it is still difficult for the non-specialist to get a wrap on some of the more weird aspects of quantum physics. This review will attempt a dumbed-down interpretation of my own tenuous grasp of what Hawking and Mlodinow are saying.

Hawking and Mlodinow are very smart guys, for sure, and they know lots and lots about physics. As I understand their presentation, we exist in a universe that is just one of an unimaginable number of universes (10^{500}) that have been created spontaneously and simultaneously out of *gravity*. Out of so many universes, it is highly likely that at least one of them would support life, and we just happen to be in that one (or one of those). In this context, it should not surprise us that the universe we are in should look like it was designed especially for us and our understanding.

This vision constitutes what Hawking/Mlodinow identify as "M-theory," which stands for the idea of multiple universes (or a "multiverse.")

The authors make interesting and provocative claims, such as: "the universe does not have just a single existence or history, but rather every possible version of the universe exists simultaneously in what is called a quantum superposition." And this "has passed every experimental test to which it has ever been subjected."

What I get out of this is that just about anything is possible somewhere in the universe or somewhere in the multiverse, because different sets of laws would pertain, depending on where you were (if, in fact, you could exist at all). What is certain, however, is that the reality of God is unnecessary to explain any of this.

I'll concede that the authors unfold in entertaining fashion a vision of "how" things came to be, but I am not at all convinced that they have handled the "why" questions very well at all ("why is there something rather than nothing," "why are we here?") What I did notice is that along the way, Hawking/Mlodinow resort (rather typically, in discussions of this sort) to rather unscientific concepts, like "luck," "lucky," and "good fortune" when addressing the apparent "fine-tuning" of our universe to the support of intelligent, carbon-based life. We've seen all that before, from lesser minds than Hawking's. But where does it all come from in the first place? Hawking's and Mlodinow's answer is gravity, which seems to be an ultimate, eternally existing reality that allows something to proceed from nothing. That gravity is a "something," however, seems to be skipped over, and "why" there should be *that* power is not explained.

It is the given law, eternally and absolutely existing. "Because there is a law like gravity, the universe can and will create itself from nothing. Spontaneous creation is the reason there is something rather than nothing, why the universe exists, why we exist."

But this is not the sense in which human beings ask these existential questions, which come from meditation on the human condition. This rootedness of the "why" question provides the context for the significance of the question in the first place, but the authors seem not to recognize or even realize this. The authors here smuggle a "how" in as an explanation of a "why" question, all the time rather arrogantly declaring that "philosophy is dead." Their final shot at this is to say that "we human beings . . . are ourselves mere collections of fundamental particles of nature." But we already have that from Bertrand Russell and Jacques Monod, *et. al.* It's just that now, with *The Grand Design,* we get it with less pathos, accompanied rather by some amusing cartoons, colorful pictures, and some very flat attempts at humor in the narrative.

Appendix II

Book Review
Quarks, Chaos, and Christianity (New York, Crossroad, 1994)
by John Polkinghorne

Review by Richard Terrell

John Polkinghorne is currently an international "star" in the Christianity-and-science conversation. Formerly a physicist and Professor of Mathematical Physics at Cambridge and now an Anglican priest, Polkinghorne's perspectives promise to bring reconciliation to the alleged "warfare" between religion and science and show how unnecessary the perceived tensions are. In this book, Polkinghorne discusses a wide range of topics, from evolution to prayer, drawing upon the ideas emerging from the strange and fascinating world of quantum physics.

Polkinghorne, while praising science as a way of knowing, is quick to point out that science works in subtle ways and involves both objectivity and subjectivity, or what he refers to as "science's successful mixture of fact and opinion." This mixture tells us something about how we acquire knowledge, and the proceedings of this mixture tell us something about how we get knowledge in other areas as well, including religion. As for religion, Polkinghorne affirms—and properly so—that if religious faith is to be of any value it must express what is actually true. "It's not a technique for whistling in the dark to keep our spirits up."

The author states the issue between Christian faith and scientific materialism clearly, pointing out that the materialist outlook gravitates toward a reductionism that is inadequate to explain universal human experience:

> Throughout the world, and throughout history, there is impressive human testimony to encounters with a Reality, both beyond us and yet also nearer to us than breathing, of one who meets humanity with judgement and mercy.
>
> Reductionists will try to explain away these non-scientific aspects of human experience. . . . For this account, music really *is* just vibrations in the air; the *Mona Lisa* really *is* just a collection of specks of paint of known chemical composition. Ethical intentions and religious intimations are just strategies for survival, programmed into us by the selfish genes. It is hard to exaggerate the implausibility of this limited view of reality. All that is most profound, all that makes human life worth living, is devalued and discarded, sacrificed to an unjustified scientific imperialism.

Neither science nor religion deals simply with pure fact or with mere opinion. Each bases its conclusions on the interplay between interpretation and experience. Because Christianity is a faith grounded in historical claims, the rational investigation of Christian truth claims is kin to scientific inquiry. In both cases of Christianity and science, there are features that are unknown, open to question, and some of which are beyond the ability of human beings to directly test. As for the totalistic, evolutionistic worldview's pretentions, Polkinghorne makes the pointed observation that "[n]early all that makes life worth living slips through the wide meshes of the scientific net."

Materialists, of course, would discard Polkinghorne's perspective on what music and art are for them. Yet, the author is not writing so much about how a materialist might respond to music and art, but what, in the final analysis, the materialist's philosophy adds up to (or reduces to). This puts the materialist "in the dock," and poses the question as to how he/she would explain the great disparity between what the materialist experiences through the arts and what those occasions actually amount to according to the philosophy. This recalls a challenge that was posed years ago by the evangelical writer Francis Schaeffer, who admitted that materialists could have a great appreciation and enthusiasm for the arts, but they could not do so in consistency with the materialist philosophy.

While materialists might argue with Polkinghorne over his assessment of their attitudes toward art and music, people with traditional theology might be uncomfortable with his attempt to weave theology and evolution together. Polkinghorne's theology is a variety of "theistic evolution" that comes pretty close, in my assessment, to just another brand of evolutionism glazed with some theological language. As such, his book is not likely to foster the kind of reconciliation between science and religion that he seeks. This is not so much the result of what he actually says but of what he overlooks.

While the author gives proper due to a theology that acknowledges God's creation of a world that is "able to make itself" (through the working of natural laws that guide its processes) one gets the impression that Polkinghorne overlooks something crucial from the standpoint of biblical theology, and that is the concept of "the Fall." Polkinghorne writes as if to suggest that nature is precisely the way God meant it to be. The evils of the world are the "inescapable cost" of designing a world "allowed to be other than God, released from tight divine control, and permitted to be itself." One might reconcile this description with the theological doctrine of the "curse," of a creation "subjected to futility," but one is left wondering what he actually means. While all Christian believers would agree that the evil of the world is the result of the world's freedom, Polkinghorne suggests that the present system of things is pretty much in accord with God's original vision, and that the world is in fact progressing toward God in the end. When he considers the role of Christ in all of this, one cannot help noting his glaring omission of any mention of Christ's death as an atonement for sin, or of his resurrection as an eschatological event heralding the promise and evidence of a "new heaven and earth" that will be released from "subjection to futility" and "its bondage to decay" (Rom. 8).

While stating Christ's death as evidence of God's love and willingness to share in our sufferings, the atonement does not figure in Polkinghorne's considerations. Why? I believe it is because it is problematic to his acceptance of evolution as that concept and vision is presented in conventional terms by scientific materialism itself. And herein lies the problem for concepts of "theistic evolution." One may breezily state that evolution in the neo-Darwinian sense is just the methodology of God's creative action, but in doing so one accepts the notion that the world exists in accord with the original creative intentions of God—a premise that bumps up against traditional Christian understandings. It may be possible to reconcile evolutionary ideas with Christian theology, but it cannot be done so easily as proposed by John Polkinghorne or others who dress up doctrines of progress with theological language. Such reconciliation would have to clarify the reality of "sin" —not just suffering and trouble—and acknowledge that Christ's death and resurrection was much more than just a signal that God is with us despite all, but that it lays the foundation for the new creation. And yes, we understand that literally, as pertaining not only to individual life but that of the whole cosmos.

John Polkinghorne is an important voice in the religion-science conversation, but this book is likely to leave both sides unsatisfied that his proposals for reconciliation are sound.

Appendix III

Book Review
The Creation-Evolution Struggle (Cambridge, Mass., Harvard
University Press, 2005)
by Michael Ruse

Review by Richard Terrell

Michael Ruse is one of the most interesting writers on the issues of science-and-religion writing today. This book rivals another masterful work—Ronald Numbers' *The Creationists*—in defining the history and intellectual context for understanding our society's ongoing controversies over evolutionism and religious faith. Ruse seeks to explain why "we have today two violently opposing camps." He seeks to do this by putting "evolution in context, particularly the context of religion itself, before and after the appearance of the *Origin*."

Ruse is careful and consistent in drawing a distinction between evolution*ism* and the biological science of evolution. He sees Darwin himself as positing, and hoping for, a genuine science of natural change, a goal that was distorted by historical forces that framed the appearance of *The Origin of Species* in 1859. In Ruse's account, the Victorian society of mid-century England was energized by notions of social progress, and many people were looking for, and hoping for, a ground of support from biological science. Evolutionary thought was, "like phrenology . . . a vehicle for pushing doctrines of progress." The evolutionary idea of progress recognized the creation of organisms by lawful means, and was embraced by British deists as a proof of God's existence. They saw life as progressing "upward," perhaps even going beyond the present form of humanity. Evolution was "a familiar fixture on the intellectual and popular landscape," and even among religious groups "there was no united wall of opposition to the kinds of thinking that evolution represented."

Darwin, in publishing his groundbreaking book, hoped for a genuine professional science. Ruse holds that Darwin's approach to evolution was modest and restrained in its goals. Nevertheless, it was difficult to shake free of the ideology of evolutionism. Darwin's theory gave impetus to the pre-existing (unscientific) notions of evolution tied to doctrines of progress.

Natural history museums built in London and New York City became cathedrals or temples for instructing the masses in the tenets of evolutionism. . . . Generations of schoolchildren were shipped in to learn about nutrition, cleanliness—and about evolution. In the process they got a large dose of instruction in the ideology of progress.

In Darwin's wake, the progressive-evolutionary vision drew upon the new biology, and its proponents began to apply it to a total understanding of cosmic origins and all aspects of human society, government, economics, and art. The vision of "simple into the complex, through successive differentiations" became the universal law of life. This view of things was sustained in the "social Darwinism" of Herbert Spencer and the "showmanship" of Darwinist propagandists like T.H. Huxley. Whatever Charles Darwin's individual intentions may have been for his theory (and Ruse is careful to protect Darwin on this point), post-Darwinian evolutionism became as much a religious vision as its pre-Darwinian predecessor. Further, "[s]trengthening the case of the religious nature of post-Darwinian evolutionism was its link to millennial thinking." As apocalyptic premillenialism weakened as an eschatological vision among Christians, postmillenialism increased—the idea of human progress promising to bring in the realization of human hopes. Thus, religious vision became wedded to biology.

Ruse gets to the core of the modern, so-called "conflicts between religion and science" in his description of "popular evolution" as offering "a world picture, a story of origins, and a special place for humans in the scheme of things," delivering moral exhortations and "prescribing what we ought to do if we want things to continue well (or to be redeemed and a decline reversed)." Evolution puts itself in a direct competition with Christianity when it focuses "on the status and obligations of humans."

Ruse is critical of the "frenzied polemics" of writers like Richard Dawkins who equate, as a necessary perspective, atheism as the proper response to biological knowledge. "Who can deny that evolution functions as more than just a scientific theory in Richard Dawkins's worldview?" he asks. "For Dawkins, contemplation of the natural world through the eyes of science is a religious experience." Nor is the tendency to make a secular religion of evolution confined to fringe extremists. The "quasi-religious commitment to evolutionism" is deeply grounded in the thinking of outstanding leaders of the discipline (e.g. William Hamilton and Edward O. Wilson).

> This holds true in England and even more so in America. In this sense, evolutionary biology— Darwinian evolutionary biology—continues to function as a kind of secular religion. It offers a story of origins. It provides a privileged place at the top for humans. It exhorts humans to action, on the basis of evolutionary principles. It opposes other solutions to questions of social behavior and morality. And it points to a brighter future if all is done as it should be done, in accordance with evolutionary theory.

Ruse's approach to the issues has earned him the suspicious eyebrow treatment from many in the world of Darwinian science. Not only is his approach considerate of perspectives that come from disciplines of inquiry outside the natural sciences, but Ruse actively engages in respectful dialogue (in this book and elsewhere) with serious creationist thinkers and enthusiasts of the Intelligent Design movement. I would guess that his major offense, though, is setting forth an argument that actually tends to support a charge often made by fundamentalist-creationist activists who have argued, over many years now, that the nation's public schools, through their approach to science instruction, have been engaged in a process of inculcating children into a secular religion grounded in evolution. What we see today, according to Ruse, is not a simple battle of fact and truth. "It is rather a struggle for the hearts and souls of people, with deep implications for the ways in which we live our lives and regulate our conduct. It is a religious or metaphysical battle, not simply a dispute about scientific theory."

Sources Cited

Barbour, Ian G., *Issues In Science and Religion*. New York: Harper Torchbooks, 1971.

Barbour, Ian G., *Myths, Models, and Paradigms*. New York: Harper and Row, 1974.

Elmer Barnes, Harry Elmer, *An Intellectual and Cultural History of the Western World*, 3 vol. New York: Dover Publications, 1965.

Behe, Michael, *The Edge of Evolution*. New York: Free Press, 2007.

Berlinski, David, *The Devil's Delusion: Atheism and Its Scientific Pretensions*. New York: Crown Forum, 2008.

Bernal, J.D., *The Origin of Life*. Cleveland: World Publishing Co., 1967.

Blum, Harold F., *Time's Arrow and Evolution*. New Jersey: Princeton University Press, 3rd edition; orig. pub. 1951.

Brace, Richard M., *The Making of The Modern World*. New York: Holt, Rinehart and Winston, 2nd edition, 1961.

Bube, Richard H., *The Human Quest*. Waco,Tex.: Word, 1971.

Coppedge, James F., *Evolution: Possible or Impossible.* Grand Rapids: Zondervan,1973.

Darwin, Charles, *Origin of Species.* London: J.M. Dent and Sons, EVERYMAN'S LIBRARY edition, 1967.

Davidheiser, Bolton, *Evolution and Christian Faith.* Presbyterian and Reformed, 1968.

Dawkins, Richard, *The God Delusion.* Boston: Houghton Mifflin, 2006.

Denton, Michael, *Evolution: A Theory in Crisis.* Bethesda, Md.: Adler and Adler, 1986.

Denton, Michael, *Nature's Destiny: How The Laws of Biology Reveal Purpose in the Universe.* New York: The Free Press, 1998

Dobzhansky, Theodosius, *Evolution, Genetics, and Man.* New York: John Wiley and Sons, Inc., 1955.

Dubay, Thomas, *The Evidential Power of Beauty: Science and Theology Meet.* San Francisco: Ignatius, 1999.

Durant, John, ed., *Darwin and Divinity.* Oxford: Basil Blackwell,1985.

Eisely, Loren, *The Immense Journey.* New York: Random House, 1957; orig. pub. 1946.

Flew, Anthony, with Varghese, Roy Abraham, *There Is A God: How The World's Most Notorious Atheist Changed His Mind.* New York: HarperCollins, 2007.

Flint, Richard F., and Skinner, Brian J., *Physical Geology.* New York: John Wiley and Sons, 1974.

Gilkey, Langdon, *Religion and The Scientific Future.* New York: Harper and Row, 1970.

Gillispie, Charles C., *Genesis and Geology*. New York: Harper Torchbooks, 1951.

Gould, Stephen Jay, *I Have Landed: The End of a Beginning In Natural History*. New York: Three Rivers Press, 2003.

Harris, Harris, *The End of Faith*. New York: W.W. Norton and Company, 2004.

Hawking, Stephen, *The Grand Design*. New York: Bantam Books, 2010.

Huxley, Julian, *Evolution in Action*. New York: Harper and Row, 1953; Signet 1957.

Huxley, Julian, *Religion Without Revelation*. New York: New American Library, 1957; Mentor edition 1958.

Jaki, Stanley L., *The Road of Science and the Ways To God*. Chicago: University of Chicago, 1978.

Jaki, Stanley L., *The Savior of Science*. Washington, D.C.: Regnery Gateway, 1988.

Koestler, Arthur, *The Act of Creation*. New York: Macmillan; Dell paperback edition, 1967.

Kerkut, G.A., *Implications of Evolution*. New York: Pergamon Press, 1960

Lewis, C.S., *Christian Reflections*. Grand Rapids: Eerdmans, 1967.

Mackay, Donald M., *The Clockwork Image*. Downers Grove, Ill., 1974.

Miller, Kenneth R., *Finding Darwin's God*. New York: Harper Perennial Books, 2002.

Monod, Jacques, *Chance and Necessity,* trans. by Austryn Wainhouse. New York: Alfred A. Knopf, 1971.

Myer, Stephen C., *Signature in the Cell.* New York: HarperCollins, 2009.

Oparin, A.I., *Origin of Life.* New York: Dover Publications, 1953.

Oparin, A.I., *The Chemical Origin of Life.* Springfield, Ill.: Charles C. Thomas Publisher, 1964.

Polkinghorne, John, *Quarks, Chaos, and Christianity.* New York: Crossroad, 2002.

Ramm, Bernard, *The Christian View of Science and Scripture.* Grand Rapids: Eerdmans, 1954.

Reid, James, *God, the Atom, and the Universe.* Grand Rapids: Zondervan, 1968.

Rifkin, Jeremy, *Algeny.* New York: The Viking Press, 1983.

Ruse, Michael, *The Creation-Evolution Controversy.* Cambridge: Harvard University Press, 2005.

Schaeffer, Francis, *He is There and He is Not Silent.* Wheaton,Ill.: Tyndale House, 1972.

Sears, Paul B., *Charles Darwin.* New York: Charles Scribner's Sons, 1950.

Simpson, George Gaylord. *This View of Life.* New York: Harcourt, Brace and World, 1964.

Smith, Christian, ed., *The Secular Solution: Power, Interests, and Conflict in the Secularization of American Public Life.* Berkeley: University of California Press, 2003.

Stark, Rodney, *For the Glory of God.* Princeton, N.J.: Princeton University Press, 2003.

Tipler, Frank J., *The Physics of Christianity.* New York: Doubleday, 2007.

Wells, Jonathan, *Icons of Evolution.* Washington, D.C.: Regnery, 2000.

Wilder-Smith, A.E., *The Creation of Life: A Cybernetic Approach to Evolution.* Wheaton, Ill.: Harold Shaw, 1970.

Witham, Larry, *By Design.* San Francisco: Encounter Books, 2003.

Articles

Bethell, Tom, "Darwin's Mistake," *Harpers* (February, 1976): 72.

Carrier, Richard, "Our Meaning in Life," *The Secular Web* (http://www.secweb.infidels.org/?kiosk=articles&id=113).

Carrier, Richard, "Are The Odds Against the Origin of Life Too Great To Accept?" (http://www.infidels.org/library/modern/richard_carrier/addenaB/html).

"Fraudulent report at AAAS and the 1986 Oxford University Debate," (http://samizat.qc.ca/origines/debate_gc.htm).

Hitching, Francis, "Was Darwin Wrong," *Life* magazine (April, 1982).

Ingalls, Albert, "The Carboniferous Mystery," *Scientific American,* January, 1940, CLXII, 14.

Morse, Gardiner, "Why Is Sex?" in *Chicago Tribune* (Section 4, Sunday January 6, 1985) 1.

Moore, William, "The Primate Fossil 'Ida': The Science and the Hype," (http://www.wsws.org/articles/2009/jun2009/ida-j13.shtml) June 13, 2009.

Holmes III, Ralston, "Shaken Atheism: A Look at the Fine-Tuned Universe," *Christian Century* (December 3, 1986), 1094.

"Professors as Suppressors," *Newsweek*, July 3, 1950, 15..

Ruse, Michael, "Saving Darwinism from the Darwinians," *National Post,* May 13, 2000, B-3.

About the Author

Richard Terrell is Emeritus Professor of Art at Doane College in Crete, Nebraska. He taught in the areas of fine arts and humanities for 44 years, first at Blackburn College, Carlinville, Illinois (1965-1970) and at Doane (1970-2009). He received the BFA degree from Illinois Wesleyan University, Bloomington, Illinois (1962) and the MFA degree from the University of Wisconsin, Madison (1964). He pursued additional studies in theology, church history, and Christian apologetics at Trinity Evangelical Divinity School, Deerfield, Illinois. He credits the integrated humanities course at Illinois Wesleyan (1958-1962) with opening his eyes to the vision and possibilities of interdisciplinary learning and the power of the Liberal Arts.

Mr. Terrell is a practicing and exhibiting visual artist. His articles on the arts and Christianity have been published in *Christianity Today, Eternity, Christianity and the Arts,* and *Christianity and Society.* He was guest editor for the May, 2001 edition of *Christianity and the Arts,* which focused on issues of popular culture, and was a contributing author to the Leland Ryken edited collection *The Christian Imagination* (2002). His first book, *Resurrecting the Third Reich* was published in 1994 by Huntington House Publishers, Lafayette, La. A related book, *Christ, Faith, and the Holocaust,* was published by Wesbow Press (Indianapolis, IN) in 2010.

Richard Terrell is program director for Ad Lib, a retreat ministry for Christian artists, writers, and performers meeting annually in Colorado. He lives in Lincoln, Nebraska, with his wife, Louise. They have two grown children and one granddaughter.